the wisdom of the
IRISH

ONEWORLD TITLES OF INTEREST

Ireland: A Short History, Joe Coohill, ISBN 1–85168–238–4
The Wisdom of the Ancient Greeks, ISBN 1–85168–298–8
The Wisdom of the Arabs, ISBN 1–85168–283–X
The Wisdom of Buddhism, ISBN 1–85168–226–0
The Wisdom of the Confucians, ISBN 1–85168–259–7
The Wisdom of Hinduism, ISBN 1–85168–227–9
The Wisdom of Jesus, ISBN 1–85168–225–2
The Wisdom of Judaism, ISBN 1–85168–228–7
The Wisdom of the Kabbalah, ISBN 1–85168–297–X
The Wisdom of the Qur'an, ISBN 1–85168–224–4
The Wisdom of Sikhism, ISBN 1–85168–280–5
The Wisdom of Sufism, ISBN 1–85168–260–0
The Wisdom of the Tao, ISBN 1–85168–232–5
The Wisdom of Zen, ISBN 1–85168–281–3

the wisdom of the
IRISH

a concise anthology

compiled by
suheil bushrui

with a foreword by brendan kennelly

ONEWORLD
OXFORD

the wisdom of the irish

Oneworld Publications
(Sales and Editorial)
185 Banbury Road
Oxford OX2 7AR
England
www.oneworld-publications.com

© Oneworld Publications 2004

ISBN 1–85168–351–8

Cover design by Design Deluxe
Printed and bound in India by Thomson Press Ltd

Dedicated to Dr C. D. Mote, Jr
President, University of Maryland
College Park
In recognition of his outstanding leadership
in promoting the dialogue of civilisations.

I give you thanks and love, as due
To all of truth that is as true
As you, good friend, and best of men
That was, is, or may be again.

James Stephens

contents

Art and Literature

Ethics

Daily Life

Forging a Nation

fOREWORÒ

by BRENÒan kennelly

This book of Irish wisdom is the work of an avid reader, scrupulous scholar and thoughtful anthologist. Suheil Bushrui has been studying Irish life and literature for several decades and has acquired a personal, unique knowledge of the culture of Ireland. As an Arab, he enjoys and explores a special perspective on Irish culture. Sometimes, an interested outsider can see things more clearly than an impassioned insider. And it is precisely that fresh, detached perspective, together with a deep knowledge of Irish life and literature, that makes this book of wisdom such an intellectual and emotional experience. It is a book that readers will return to again and again because it is full of verbal jewels that shine in the darkness of the heart and mind.

In the strict sense, Ireland lacks the kind of sustained philosophical tradition that one finds in many countries throughout the world. Instead, we find poets, dramatists, novelists, singers, talkers and storytellers in rich abundance all through the island. And Suheil Bushrui, being the ever-hungry reader and gifted listener that he is, has explored that world of proverbs, sayings, songs, poems, political declarations, plays, epigrams, popular rhymes, translations, prefaces, stray notes, historical compilations, sermons, ballads, recorded conversations and many other sources with the blend of passion, discipline and detachment that one finds only in the work of the most accomplished scholars. A considerable part of the attractiveness of this book is due to what I can only call the music of the wisdom collected here. There are moments when the pages seem to sing their wisdom in a spirit of celebration and joy. Strange, when you consider the sadness and pain of so much Irish history. But perhaps there is a sense in which time and language turn pain, sadness and grief into musical, singing wisdom. We are all indebted to Suheil Bushrui for giving us this priceless gift.

introduction

In an essay entitled 'A Visit to America', Dylan Thomas refers to those promoters of things Irish as 'professional Irishmen'.[1] Whether this description applies also to himself or not, it is certain that this Welsh poet discharged with competence and relish his 'professionalism' in promoting the Celtic tradition, be it Irish or Welsh. I, on the other hand, regard myself as an 'adopted son of Ireland', coming from outside both the English and the native Irish traditions. My 'Ireland' is not the Ireland of historians, of literary critics, of political scientists, of archaeologists, of folklorists, or of anthropologists; my Ireland is that Ireland of the Imagination which my late friend Kathleen Raine described as follows:

> I was a child of my time and had long loved what I can only call the Ireland of the Imagination. By this I do not mean that this Ireland, whose existence is invisible, discoverable only in its music, story, mythology, speech and language, was or is, 'imaginary', in the sense of being unreal. On the contrary, that inner country, distilled by every nation in the form of its arts – a certain incommunicable essence that can be experienced but never analysed – is more real, certainly in the sense that concerns poets more 'real', than the geographical or political country. It is what remains when historic

actuality is forgotten. For this quintessence of the inner life of a people is the expression of some one among the many modes of the human spirit, which we call France, or Spain, or Japan, or Russia – or indeed England; although the laborious task of secreting that essence obscures from day to day that inner quality of our own country, whatever it may be. Most of us have perhaps some secret inner nationality – or several – be it ancient Egypt or ancient Greece, or India, or Japan – countries we have known only through their imaginative expressions. ... I shared with the Irish that strong sense of an older loyalty to a vanished kingdom and with that an intensive love of a landscape of the heart to which the Imagination is wedded – something Yeats understood as the ground of every oral tradition: 'Have not all races had their first unity from a mythology that marries them to rock and hill?' Yeats asks.[2]

Yes, indeed, it is that 'landscape of the heart' that spoke to me when I embarked some forty years ago on my pilgrimage towards that Holy City, that island of 'saints and scholars'. It was Holy Ireland, her spiritual tradition and perennial wisdom that captured my imagination.

Looking back, however, I recognise the enormous debt I owe to one single book that fanned into flame my passion for study and research. It was not only my first encounter with things Irish, but it also provided the inspiration for everything I have done in the service of Irish culture, in either English or Arabic.

The book was entitled *The Genius of Ireland*, written by George Townshend and published in 1930. The last paragraph of the second essay, which gave the book its title, emphasised Ireland's contribution to the future of civilisation, a contribution that is none other than Ireland's rare capacity for spiritual attainment and moral leadership.

The Genius of Ireland became a sacred book for me and led me to discover through the study of Irish literature and civilisation a whole universe of learning, not of discursive reason but of the Imagination. I entered the world of a great living mystery in which all things spoke of unity. With George Townshend as my guide I began to explore Irish literature. I searched for that 'gift of spiritual sensibility' in Irish legend and folk literature, from the myths of

Cuchulain to the plays of the Abbey Theatre, but above all in the works of my literary master, William Butler Yeats. In all this I came to discover the ecstasy of imaginative revelation. I rejected the pride of acquired knowledge and celebrated instead the humility of the true scholar, aware of the limitations of the intellect before the majesty of the timeless and the sanctity of Truth.

Ireland did not only claim my mind. It also claimed my heart through the generosity and warmth of its people, who bestowed their love and friendship on me. I can never forget the warm welcome and kind, encouraging words of President Eamon de Valera in the summer of 1971 when I presented him with my book, *Images and Memories: A Pictorial Record of the Life and Work of W. B. Yeats,*[3] on behalf of the American University of Beirut, Lebanon, where we had established the first Centre for Irish Studies in the Arab world.

The President's words to me on that occasion struck a deep chord and seemed to emphasise once more what George Townshend had already impressed upon me:

> We were not fighting for political freedom alone. We wanted to build up a community in which an ever increasing number of its members would be free to devote themselves more and more to the mind and spirit. Ireland could then become again, as it was for centuries in the past, a great intellectual and missionary centre from which would go forth the satisfying saving truths of Divine Revelation, as well as the fruits of the ripest secular knowledge.

President de Valera was then in his late eighties, but my meeting with him left an indelible impression on my mind. The dignity of the man said it all; gracious, serene and extremely courteous. He treated me with a respect that reflected his greatness as a leader. He showed considerable interest in the work we were doing in the Arab world in the early seventies. It seemed to me then, as it does now almost thirty-four years later, that I was in the presence of a deeply religious and spiritual man. There was something mystical about him; he was a teacher in every sense of the word, but above all I saw him as the father of the nation. There was an aura of honesty about him that transcended the barriers of both protocol and diplomacy, and an integrity that welled out of his very being. In many ways he represented all those remarkable traits of the Irish character: infinite delicacy of sentiment, charming modesty, unobtrusive eloquence, and self–effacing poise. Yet beneath his suave manner one could not ignore his indomitable spirit and an iron will that was fearless and invincible.

But this sense of Ireland and of the Irish which I have gleaned from the people I have met and the literature I have read was greatly intensified by friendships founded on collaborative efforts in the service of Irish culture: the late Sir Desmond Cochrane; Yvonne Lady Cochrane; Sir Marc and Lady Cochrane; two distinguished Irish Ambassadors serving in the Arab world during the seventies and eighties, namely Eamon Ó Tuathail and Gearóid Ó Clérigh; and last but not least, my able and erudite publisher, Colin Smythe. Nor can I forget the many Irish friends I found through my membership of IASAIL (The International Association for the Study of Anglo-Irish Literature) of which I had the honour to be Chairman from 1985 to 1988. I am eternally indebted to the omniscient, Gaelic-speaking scholar, Robert Welch, for his assiduous efforts in helping me to expand the international activities of the Association during my tenure. Nor can I ignore the profound impression left on me by the work of two eminent scholars, Seán Ó Tuama, and the poet Thomas Kinsella, who dedicated their book, *An Duanaire, 1600–1900: Poems of the Dispossessed* in the following words, 'For Suheil Bushrui, a gentleman (I hear), with a nuclear family and a singular wife', signed Seán Ó Tuama; and 'For them all, with everything', signed Thomas Kinsella. This has been a gift that I have cherished over the years and a book that I have read more than once. It was at IASAIL also that I met Brendan Kennelly, one of Ireland's most distinguished poets. He and I shared a faith in the redeeming power of poetry, and his voice has always seemed to me to capture in its modernity the noble values of the ancient bards.

In the West of Ireland, particularly the Yeats Country around Sligo, I found my true spiritual home. My first visit to Ireland was in 1960 when the First International Yeats Summer School was founded; I was among the founding students of that institution, which still is in existence. It was there that I also forged lasting friendships with the internationally renowned Oxford poet Francis Warner; John Kelly, the editor of Yeats's letters; Terence Brown, the brilliant author of the first book to trace the progress of poetry in Ulster; the historian Kevin Nolan; the Nobel Laureate Seamus Heaney, to whose influence I am greatly indebted; and the late senator and astute literary critic, Augustine Martin. It was at the Summer School that I met the two brothers, Tom and John Mullaney of Sligo. Tom, sadly, passed away a few years ago, but John, thank God, is still with us. For me, these two brothers represented what is best in Ireland and symbolised what the gentleman scholar should be like.

The Sligo countryside with the towering mountains of Ben Bulben (the Peak of Gulba) and Knocknarea (the Hill of the Storms) represented for me an invisible world that was only experienced by those who share the vision of the Unity of Being. In the West of Ireland I came to recognise kindred spirits who communicated with that 'landscape of the heart': the poets of Ireland from Amergin, the first of the bards, to Yeats, Ireland's greatest poet and one of the great poets of all time. In their voices I heard the divine Sufi poets of my own Arab tradition, and the spiritual bond between myself and the Irish became meaningful and strong.

*   *   *

Ireland is a small country whose problems have raised issues of major importance, socially and politically, with regard to Europe and the world. Situated on the periphery of the European continent, Ireland's geographic position protected her racial integrity, but did not prevent wave after wave of invaders from conquering the land; Norsemen, Anglo-Normans, Scottish and English invaders settled there. Instead of changing Ireland, these newcomers were themselves changed by Ireland. In time, the invaders were 'Irishised' and turned into patriots who sought, with the majority Gaelic population, to liberate their 'homeland'. The history of Ireland is intensely turbulent: almost seven hundred years of British rule; eight major armed rebellions; a Jacobite war; the persecution of Catholics and dissenters, denying them basic human rights and dispossessing them of land and property – amounting, indeed, to nothing less than systematic exploitation; wide-scale evictions; a major disaster known as the Great Famine or Great Hunger (1845–8); a de facto partition of Ireland under the leadership of Sir Edward Carson in 1913 in the North; a bloody Civil War (1922–3); and finally wide–scale emigration of the young, the able and the productive who left their country to seek a better life elsewhere, but mainly in North America.

In the midst of such horrific circumstances and flagrant injustices suffered by the majority of the people of Ireland, the Irish entertained hope against all hope, and in the face of misery, deprivation, hunger and destitution, they remained resolute in search of their identity. Irish everywhere found themselves confronted and assailed above all with regard to their native tongue and their Catholic faith. Political Ireland had failed to provide the country with a definite identity and hence remained ineffectual in protecting or promoting the interests of the nation. But when political activity was at its lowest ebb after the death of Charles Stewart Parnell in 1891, it was the Ireland of the Imagination that defined national identity and thereby provided the vigour and the success of the social and political endeavours of the nation.

Although the Irish literary renaissance was a non-political movement, it was nevertheless national in the true sense of the word, deriving its dynamic force from Ireland's spiritual and intellectual heritage. It inspired the nation in its search for its identity: it explored its immemorial past, recreated its myth and legend, retrieved the fresh liberal breath of its Christian tradition and vivified the native language through a prodigious effort of translating Gaelic literature into English. It also expressed in a new language, 'Anglo-Irish', a vision of national unity and religious amity. This remarkable feat of literature allied itself with nationalism that was outside the realm of politics but which in time served the highest moral and ethical principles of Ireland's political life. It was as though 'the Celtic spirit, imprisoned in the shell of an almost extinct language and obscured by the dust of political turmoil,' was set free.[4] Although there was opposition and bitter quarrelling about what was national and what was not, this did not change the fact that the leaders who announced in 1916 the creation of the Republic of Ireland represented in every sense of the word the Irish nation as a whole. They were Catholics and Protestants, of Gaelic and non-Gaelic descent, who were united in one cause and who created a vision that finally brought into being an independent Ireland.

* * *

The political climate of Ireland left deep scars on the people, and the bitter conflict of a small nation with the mightiest empire of the time made nationality the first consideration of all Irish people. It also imposed upon them – in addition to those unmistakably Irish legendary gifts of a fertile imagination, a sharp sense of humour and enchanting eloquence – a certain belligerence and a degree of wariness towards those whom they do not know well.

The nature of the conflict between England and Ireland was such that each side tried to dehumanise the other. The press, though, was overwhelmingly English, and the literature that carried that image had its centre in London, the capital of the empire. Thus the stock character known as the stage Irishman was a buffoon whose counterpart appeared in novels and at a later date in films. It was left to G. K. Chesterton to summarise in his whimsical style the attitude of most people in England towards Ireland:

> For the great Gaels of Ireland
> Are the men that God made mad.
> For all their wars are merry,
> And all their songs are sad.

This, however, is certainly open to question, as anyone who has heard an Irish jig or a drinking song can attest.

For a long time Ireland was only associated in the minds of many people with Dublin prawns, Guinness, fairies and leprechauns, race-horses, war, religious conflict and the Blarney stone. That image began to change, however, when Ireland came into her own in 1948 as an independent republic.

By the mid-seventies, Ireland had achieved an enviable status in every human endeavour at home and abroad. The Irish participated as teachers, doctors, nurses and technical experts in helping developing countries, especially in Africa and Asia. Ireland's army became one of the most efficient and effective instruments in resolving major conflicts and in international peace-keeping. In industry, technology and, most important of all, in agriculture, the Irish contribution has been enormous. Above all, the home front saw great improvements in housing, education, health and social welfare.

In 1980 Ireland was confident enough to send to London a splendid display of Irish culture called the 'Sense of Ireland' Festival. The Festival took London by storm and the British press hailed it as the dominant cultural event on the London scene. W. L. Webb's remarks in the *Guardian* newspaper underlined not only what yesterday's impoverished colony had achieved, but also the rich and magnificent cultural world that England's closest neighbour possessed.

> Never mind the Blarney. Feel the Breadth – Whatever about a terrible beauty. Ireland has certainly changed in the last decade, and one reason for A Sense of Ireland is to tell the world all about it ... what's importantly on offer is a sense of a modern European state, her independence and ancient links with the wider world.[5]

Today Ireland is a leading member of the European Union; she has won the admiration of the whole world, and her contribution, along with that of her sons and daughters overseas, has been immensely enriching in a world rapidly moving towards globalisation.

Mary McAleese, President of Ireland, in her inaugural speech of 11 November 1997 spoke of 'the global Irish family' and stated that the theme of her presidency is 'Building Bridges'. She adds, 'These bridges require no engineering skills, but they will demand patience, imagination and courage.' But such skills are all attributes of the spirit. They are skills the world must learn in order to enhance the global society now emerging culturally, commercially and politically.

From the fifth to the ninth centuries, Ireland preserved the written treasures of the Western world; her saints and scholars were the shapers of medieval culture. They also preserved Christian civilisation and spread knowledge everywhere. Nine centuries later, and after a long history of suffering and pain, Ireland rediscovered her ancient culture and noble heritage, rooted in that unanimous and universal tradition, the perennial philosophy. In the twentieth century, through that discovery, she made enormous contributions to world culture through her art, drama, poetry, music and dance, assuming a position of influence and importance far exceeding the size of her land or population.

Now that Ireland is affluent and prosperous, with the materialist world encroaching on every aspect of Irish spiritual and cultural life, will she remember the lessons of her past? Will she, as a major force in the process of globalisation, seek her own spiritual roots and help humanity today to define our new identity as 'citizens of one world'? Will today's Ireland, inspired by her wisdom and experience, help to create the world society founded on human rights, unity in diversity, inter-faith harmony, justice and peace for all? Will she live up to the vision so eloquently expressed by George Townshend in *The Genius of Ireland* and fulfil her mission in the service of humanity at large?

> To consider that this great gift of spiritual sensibility belongs in a marked degree to the Irish: to look back on a distant past and see how the religious genius of the people made this lovely island once the shrine of Western Europe: to realise that still there burns deep in the dumb heart of the people that ancient fire: to hear to-day in our midst the voice of poets beginning to raise again the strain so long unheard, and chant in the ears of a forgetful world the praise of eternal beauty and eternal truth: thus to watch, to listen, and to reflect is to be filled with hope that Ireland may not be slow to catch

the vision of a breaking day, or to hear the tidings already breathed from on high, and that she may do for mankind now such service as her saints and scholars did for Europe long ago.[6]

To compile an anthology on the 'wisdom of the Irish' is to have it borne in upon one that the literature in question expresses in essence the same 'perennial philosophy' that forms the common heritage of all races, albeit seen from the unique perspective of the Irish people. In any such endeavour a central dilemma inevitably arises: what should we adopt as the criteria for selection? The difficulty is compounded here by the sheer richness of Irish literature.

I use the word 'Irish' here without restricting the meaning of the word to any narrow racial or linguistic sense; I have tried to represent the tradition of wisdom of the whole country. It is only prudent, however, to admit that it has been impossible within the scope of this book to represent the tradition in an adequate way. In putting this anthology together I have no theory to vindicate, no policy to defend. I am neither Irish nor European; I come from outside both the Irish and the English traditions, and my response to Ireland's cultural heritage is as objective as can be expected, but the selection of passages is necessarily personal and subjective. Limitations of space and a desire to avoid as much as possible the unhappy experience of obtaining permission to include copyright material have led to the exclusion of much excellent material; in many cases, indeed, it was simply not possible even to trace the holder of the copyright.

The contents of the present work comprise passages excerpted from a variety of sources reproduced in their original form (preserving idiosyncrasies of spelling, orthography and verse arrangement) without accompanying footnotes, which I feel to be unnecessary in this context. Despite the presence in various passages of certain slight obscurities, I nevertheless felt it preferable not to spoil their integrity by burdening the reader with unnecessary explanations.

As regards the layout, the excerpts have been accompanied by just so much explanation as seemed necessary to enhance appreciation of their merits without altering the character of a work intended for the general reader. Below each passage the name of the author, when known, is provided, followed by the name of the translator in brackets. Sayings, statements, songs, ballads, blessings and aphorisms belonging to common parlance are designated by genre rather than assigned to a particular source. For ease of identification, in all poetry only the titles of poems are given. In other instances when a quotation is from a work (whether a collection of stories or legends), the titles of the books concerned are given, such as T. W. Rolleston's *Myths and Legends of the Celtic Race*, P. W. Joyce's *Old Celtic Romances*, and Lady Gregory's *Gods and Fighting Men*. These are presented consistently, even where the poems are given differently in the parent source. A full bibliography of all the various sources consulted in compiling this anthology is appended at the end of the volume.

NOTES

1. Dylan Thomas, *British and American Essays, 1905–1956*, compiled by Carl L. Anderson and George Walton Williams (New York: Holt, Rinehart and Winston, 1959).
2. Kathleen Raine, *W. B. Yeats and the Learning of the Imagination* (Ipswich, UK: Golgonooza Press, 1999), 9.
3. *Images and Memories: A Pictorial Record of the Life and Work of W. B. Yeats*, selected and edited by S. B. Bushrui and J. M. Munro (Beirut: Dar el-Mashreq, 1970).
4. Ernest Boyd, *Ireland's Literary Renaissance* (Dublin: Allen Figgis, 1969), 25.
5. W. L. Webb, *Guardian* (1 February 1980).
6. George Townshend, *The Genius of Ireland and other essays* (Dublin: Talbot Press, 1930), 51.

pROLOGUE

The word is immortal. The word continues. What has helped me to continue to write is my faith in the word. And if the word comes to an end, everything comes to an end. The word is an anchor.

Samuel Beckett, conversation with the editor

To be sure I do not deny that imagination can lead the intellect astray but I cannot conceive of an appreciation of beauty without a cultivated imagination.

Gearóid Ó Clérigh, letter to the editor, 30 December 2003

Steady under strain and strong through tension,
        Its feet on both sides but in neither camp
        It stands its ground, a span of pure attention,
        A holding action, the arches and the ramp
        Steady under strain and strong through tension.

Seamus Heaney, 'The Bridge', from 'Ten Glosses'

In order to flourish, peace needs an environment in which there is respect at all levels for other people. Creating that environment means equipping people with the mindset to recognize and accommodate the 'otherness' of others. It involves an acceptance that we are all, to some extent, blinkered by perceptions, prejudices, beliefs, and sometimes, plain misinformation. The task is to condition minds and hearts, to move towards a generous, sharing Ireland that encompasses many traditions and cultures, that creates a space for all of its people – where the richness of diversity is not just a virtue, but a profound necessity.

A healthy society is one which celebrates diversity rather than suppresses it, where cultures, creeds, and traditions draw on each other rather than try to bury each other. As we acknowledge this great reality of diversity and demand our space in it, we also need to acknowledge in our deepest being the right of all others to their space too. It behooves all of us to look at what we say, at what we practise, and at what we profess. Surely the real place for all religions is as wagers of peace, as removers of barriers and divisions. Each of us on this island should look firstly to ourselves, and then to our religion, to see if change is required and how we might make that change.

Mary McAleese, address to the Bahá'í community in Dublin,
22 April 1998

IReLANO

ANO heR

people

the celtic heartland

Erin! thy silent tear never shall cease,
   Erin! thy languid smile ne'er shall increase,
      Till, like the rainbow's light,
      Thy various tints unite,
      And form, in Heaven's sight,
         One arch of peace!

Thomas Moore, 'Erin! The Tear and the Smile in Thine Eyes'

Magical country, full of memories and dreams,
   My youth lies in the crevices of your hills;
   Here in the silk of your grass by the edge of the
      meadows,
   Every flower and leaf has its memories of you.
   Home was home then and the people friendly,
   And you and I going home in the lengthening
      shadows.

Katherine Tynan, 'The Old Country'

She is a rich and rare land;
   Oh! she's a fresh and fair land;
   She is a dear and rare land –
   This native land of mine.

No men than her's are braver –
   Her women's hearts ne'er waver;
   I'd freely die to save her,
   And think my lot divine.

She's not a dull or cold land;
   No! she's a warm and bold land;
   Oh! she's a true and old land –
   This native land of mine.

Could beauty ever guard her,
   And virtue still reward her,
   No foe would cross her border –
   No friend within it pine!

Oh, she's a fresh and fair land;
   Oh, she's a true and rare land!
   Yes, she's a rare and fair land –
   This native land of mine.

Thomas Davis, 'My Land'

And I will make my journey, if life and health but
   stand,
   Unto that pleasant country, that fresh and fragrant
     strand,
   And leave your boasted braveries, your wealth and
     high command,
      For the fair hills of holy Ireland.

Samuel Ferguson, 'The Fair Hills of Ireland'

Love of country, *tirgradh*, is I think the real passion; and bound up with it are love of home, of family, love of God.

Lady Gregory, POETS AND DREAMERS

O the Shamrock, the green, immortal Shamrock!
    Chosen leaf
    Of bard and chief,
    Old Erin's native Shamrock!

Says Valour, "See,
    They spring for me,
Those leafy gems of morning!"
    Says Love, "No, no,
    For *me* they grow,
My fragrant path adorning!"
    But Wit perceives
    The triple leaves,
And cries – "Oh! do not sever
    A type that blends
    Three godlike friends,
Love, Valour, Wit, for ever!"

O the Shamrock, the green, immortal Shamrock!
    Chosen leaf
    Of bard and chief,
    Old Erin's native Shamrock!

Thomas Moore, 'O the Shamrock!'

O Ireland, isn't it grand you look –
    Like a bride in her rich adornin'?
And with all the pent-up love of my heart
    I bid you the top of the mornin'!

John Locke, 'The Exile's Return'

'O rise up, Willy Reilly! and come along with me;
　　I mean for to go with you and leave this counterie, –
　　To leave my father's dwelling, his houses and free
　　　land:'
And away goes Willy Reilly and his dear Coolen Bawn.

'Willy Reilly,' an Ulster ballad

'Twas the dream of a God,
　　And the mould of His hand,
That you shook 'neath His stroke,
　　That you trembled and broke
To this beautiful land.

Here He loosed from His hold
　　A brown tumult of wings,
Till the wind on the sea
　　Bore the strange melody
Of an island that sings.

He made you all fair,
　　You in purple and gold,
You in silver and green,
　　Till no eye that has seen
Without love can behold.

I have left you behind
　　In the path of the past,
With the white breath of flowers,
　　With the best of God's hours,
I have left you at last.

Dora Sigerson, 'Ireland'

Let you come this day for there's no place but Ireland where the
Gael can have peace always.

J. M. Synge, DEIRDRE OF THE SORROWS

I doubt if any nation can become prosperous unless it has national faith, and one very important part of national faith is faith in its resources, faith both in the richness of its soil and the richness of its intellect, and I am convinced that as much wealth can come from the intellect of Ireland as will come from the soil and that the one will repay cultivation as much as the other.

W. B. Yeats, 'Condition of Schools', 30 March 1926

O Paddy dear, an' did ye hear the news that's goin'
    round?
  The shamrock is by law forbid to grow on Irish
    ground!
  No more Saint Patrick's Day we'll keep, his colour
    can't be seen,
  For there's a cruel law agin the wearin' o' the Green!
  I met wid Napper Tandy, and he took me by the
    hand,
  And he said, 'How's poor ould Ireland, and how
    does she stand?'
  She's the most disthressful country that iver yet was
    seen,
  For they're hangin' men an' women there for the
    wearin' o' the Green.

'The Wearin' of the Green', an Irish song

The German Palatines, the French Huguenots, the English Protestants flying from the fires of Smithfield, later the Wesleyans and the Jews, who were persecuted in every land, in this land of ours always found safe asylum. That glorious record must not be tarnished by acts against a helpless minority.

Eamon de Valera, speaking at Mullingar, 30 April 1922

Ireland, it's the one place on earth
   That heaven has kissed
   With melody, mirth,
   And meadow and mist.

An Irish blessing

For oh! were the tributes of Alba mine
   From shore unto centre, from centre to sea,
   The site of one house, to be marked by a line
   In the midst of fair Derry were dearer to me.

That spot is the dearest on Erin's ground,
   For the treasures that peace and that purity lend,
   For the hosts of bright angels that circle it round,
   Protecting its borders from end to end.

The dearest of any on Erin's ground
   For its peace and its beauty I gave it my love,
   Each leaf of the oaks around Derry is found
   To be crowded with angels from heaven above.

Attributed to St Columcille (trans. Douglas Hyde)

Where the blue eye beams with light,
   Where there is the open hand,
   Where the mood is dark and bright
   There is also Ireland.
   Welcome, Brothers, and well met
   In the Land that bids you hail:
   Far apart though we be set,
   Gael does not forget the Gael.

Oliver St John Gogarty, 'Ode'

But there is one country in Europe in which, by virtue of a marvellous strength and tenacity of the historical intellect, and of filial devotedness to the memory of their ancestors, there have been preserved down into the early phases of mediæval civilisation, and then committed to the sure guardianship of manuscript, the hymns, ballads, stories, and chronicles, the names, pedigrees, achievements, and even characters, of those ancient kings and warriors over whom those massive cromlechs were erected and great cairns piled. There is not a conspicuous sepulchral monument in Ireland, the traditional history of which is not recorded in our ancient literature, and of the heroes in whose honour they were raised. In the rest of Europe there is not a single barrow, dolmen, or cist of which the ancient traditional history is recorded; in Ireland there is hardly one of which it is not. And these histories are in many cases as rich and circumstantial as that of men of the greatest eminence who have lived in modern times. Granted that the imagination which for centuries followed with eager interest the lives of these heroes, beheld as gigantic what was not so, as romantic and heroic what was neither one nor the other, still the great fact remains, that it was beside and in connection with the mounds and cairns that this history was elaborated, and elaborated concerning them and concerning the heroes to whom they were sacred.

Standish O'Grady, EARLY BARDIC LITERATURE

Agriculture in due time will be recognised as one of the intellectual employments, needing far more brains than driving rivets or other kinds of factory work which prevail in that city of Ireland which regards itself as the centre of civilisation.

A. E., 'The Status of Agriculture', THE IRISH HOMESTEAD,
20 July 1918

And shall I ne'er again behold thee
   My infant joy, thou much-loved Isle?
   Ah, no! thy faithless sons have sold thee.

John O'Keeffe, 'My Lamentation'

Before the Williamite train reached Ballyneety
   and the Jacobites got off the boat in France
   or Cromwell called whoa! to his horse when seated
   in Drogheda under a hard hat
   or the guns and pikes of the Elizabethan
   drove Spaniard and Ulsterman down and back,
   before Norman marksmen came to Wexford's
      beaches
   for the hunting season – no numerous pack –
   or the Gaels, whose royal blood most of us chiefly
   claim, or previous half-remembered immigrants,
   already "Your Ordinary Irishman" was the people:
   torque and adzehead though lost beneath earth
      or lake these thousands of years past
   alive today the mind's matrix of their cunning
      makers,
   dark source whose depths since before Saint Patrick
   have housed coldeyed shadows, subtle salmon of
      knowledge.

Gearóid Ó Clérigh, 'Patience,'

Know, that I would accounted be
   True brother of a company
   That sang, to sweeten Ireland's wrong,
   Ballad and story, rann and song.

W. B. Yeats, 'To Ireland in the Coming Times'

the irish people

Long, long ago, beyond the misty space
    Of twice a thousand years,
  In Erin old there dwelt a mighty race,
    Taller than Roman spears;
Like oaks and towers they had a giant grace,
    Were fleet as deers,
  With wind and waves they made their 'biding place,
    These western shepherd seers.

Thomas D'Arcy McGee, 'The Celts'

We were originally Celts here with an ancient civilization and systems of law. The Norsemen and the Normen were invaders. They secured the supreme political power but, underneath, the overwhelming majority of our people – the great body of the nation – adhered to their own way of thought and preserved their original Celticity.

Eamon de Valera as quoted by Mary C. Bromage in 'Image of Nationhood'

The genius of our nation is far more prone to love than hate. There is no gospel of personal or national hate in our religion; we are told at our mothers' knees to love all men, including our enemies.

D. P. Moran, 'The Battle of Two Civilizations'

The enthusiasm with which the Irish intellect seized upon the grand moral life of Christianity, and ideals so different from, and so hostile to, those of the heroic age, did not consume the traditions or destroy the pious and reverent spirit in which men still looked back upon those monuments of their own pagan teachers and kings, and the deep spirit of patriotism and affection with which the mind still clung to the old heroic age, whose types were warlike prowess, physical beauty, generosity, hospitality, love of family and nation, and all those noble attributes which constituted the heroic character as distinguished from the saintly.

Standish O'Grady, EARLY BARDIC LITERATURE

When Irish eyes are smiling,
  Sure it's like a morning spring.
  In the lilt of Irish laughter
  You can hear the angels sing.
  When Irish hearts are happy,
  All the world seems bright and gay.
  And when Irish eyes are smiling,
  They'll steal your heart away!

'When Irish eyes are smiling', an Irish song

Wherever you go and whatever you do,
  May the luck of the Irish be there with you.

An Irish blessing

I have travelled much, and seen various parts of the world, and I think the Irish are the most virtuous nation on the face of the earth. They are a good and brave people, and had I a thousand lives, I would yield them in their service.

Thomas Russell, speech from the dock

There is still some incorruptible spiritual atom in our people. We are still in some relation to the divine order; and while that incorrupted spiritual atom still remains all things are possible if by some inspiration there could be revealed to us a way back or forward to greatness, an Irish polity in accord with national character.

A. E., 'The National Being'

Anon stood nigh
    By my side a man
Of princely aspect and port sublime.
    Him queried I –
      'O, my Lord and Khan,
What clime is this, and what golden time?'
    When he – 'The clime
    Is a clime to praise,
The clime is Erin's, the green and bland;
    And it is the time,
      These be the days,
Of Cáhal Mór of the Wine-red Hand!'

James Clarence Mangan, 'A Vision of Connaught in the Thirteenth Century'

Our Irish blunders are never blunders of the heart.

Maria Edgeworth, 'Essay on Irish Bulls'

Ireland without her people is nothing to me.

James Connolly, Workers Republic, 7 July 1900

My heart is in woe,
And my soul deep in trouble –
    For the mighty are low,
And abased are the noble.

Fearflatha Ó Gnímh, 'The Downfall of the Gael'
(trans. Samuel Ferguson)

The Gael loves to follow an idea rather than a thing, and the more shadowy and elusive the idea the greater the enchantment it lends, and he follows the ghost of his language now with outstretched arms.

George Moore, Salve

Irish poets, learn your trade,
    Sing whatever is well made, …
    Sing the lords and ladies gay
    That were beaten into the clay
    Through seven heroic centuries;
    Cast your mind on other days
    That we in coming days may be
    Still the indomitable Irishry.

W. B. Yeats, 'Under Ben Bulben'

IRISh LANGUAGE

a people without a language of its own is only half a nation. ...
A nation should guard its language more than its territories.
... To lose your native tongue, and learn that of an alien is the
worst badge of conquest – it is the chain on the soul. To have lost
entirely the national language is death; the fetter has worn
through.

*Thomas Davis as quoted by Daniel Corkery in 'Davis and the
National Language'*

Our national language has a vital role. Language is a chief
characteristic of nationhood – the embodiment, as it were,
of the nation's personality and the closest bond between its people. No nation with a language of its own would willingly abandon it. ... They know that without it they would sink into an
amorphous cosmopolitanism – without a past, or a distinguish-
able future.

Eamon de Valera, Easter 1966 message to the people of Ireland

It is through language that a tradition of thought is preserved, and so it may be said that the language is the soul of a race. It is through language that the spirit is communicated, and it is through language that a nation becomes aware of itself.

George Moore, 'Literature and the Irish Language'

If we're truly Gaelic, we must constantly discuss the question of the Gaelic revival and the question of Gaelicism. There is no use in having Gaelic, if we converse in it on non–Gaelic topics. He who speaks Gaelic but fails to discuss the language question is not truly Gaelic in his heart; such conduct is of no benefit to Gaelicism because he only jeers at Gaelic and reviles the Gaels. There is nothing in this life so nice and so Gaelic as truly true Gaelic Gaels who speak in true Gaelic Gaelic about the truly Gaelic language. … Up the Gaels! Long live the Gaelic tongue!

Flann O'Brien, THE POOR MOUTH

The words and phrases of a language are always to some extent revelations of the mind of the race that has moulded the language.

Padraic Pearse, 'The Murder Machine'

The language, which grows up with a people, is conformed to their organs, descriptive of their climate, constitution, and manners, mingled inseparably with their history, and their soil, fitted beyond any other language to express their prevalent thoughts in the most natural efficient way.

Thomas Davis, 'Our National Language', THE NATION, *1 April 1843*

Ireland alone was never even visited, much less subjugated, by the Roman legionaries, and maintained its independence against all comers nominally until the close of the twelfth century, but for all practical purposes a good three hundred years longer.

Ireland has therefore this unique feature of interest, that it carried an indigenous Celtic civilisation, Celtic institutions, art, and literature, and the oldest surviving form of the Celtic language, right across the chasm which separates the antique from the modern world, the pagan from the Christian world, and on into the full light of modern history and observation.

T. W. Rolleston, MYTHS AND LEGENDS OF THE CELTIC RACE

I place my hope on the water
    in this little boat
    of the language, the way a body might put
    an infant

in a basket of intertwined
    iris leaves,
    its underside proofed
    with bitumen and pitch,

then set the whole thing down amidst
    the sedge
    and bulrushes by the edge
    of a river

only to have it borne hither and thither,
    not knowing where it might end up;
    in the lap, perhaps,
    of some Pharaoh's daughter.

Nuala Ní Dhomhnaill, 'The Language Issue' (trans. Paul Muldoon)

In Ireland, where the Gaelic tongue is still spoken, and to some little extent where it is not, the people live according to a tradition of life that existed before commercialism, and the vulgarity founded upon it; and we who would keep the Gaelic tongue and Gaelic memories and Gaelic habits of mind would keep them, as I think, that we may some day spread a tradition of life that makes neither great wealth nor great poverty, that makes the arts a natural expression of life, that permits even common men to understand good art and high thinking, and to have the fine manners these things can give.

W. B. Yeats, 'A Postscript'

nature and the sea

She is rapt in dreams divine.
  As her clouds of beauty pass
  On our glowing hearts they shine,
  Mirrored there as in a glass.

Earth, whose dreams are we and they,
  With her deep heart's gladness fills
  All our human lips can say
  Or the dawn-fired singer trills.

A. E., 'The Golden Age'

This country of ours is no sand-bank thrown up by some recent caprice of earth. It is an ancient land, honoured in the archives of civilisation, traceable into antiquity by its piety, its valour, and its sufferings.

Thomas Davis as quoted by Frank Gallagher in 'Davis and the Modern Revolution'

h ow diverse, rich, and indispensable to happiness are the gifts
and graces of the countryside! The whole of man's being,
material and spiritual, draws sustenance from it.

George Townshend, THE GENIUS OF IRELAND

L ook! are not the fields covered with a delightful verdure? Is
there not something in the woods and groves, in the rivers
and clear springs that soothes, that delights, that transports the
soul? At the prospect of the wide and deep ocean, or some huge
mountain whose top is lost in the clouds, or of an old gloomy
forest, are not our minds filled with a pleasing horror? Even in
rocks and deserts, is there not an agreeable wildness? How sin-
cere a pleasure is it to behold the natural beauties of the earth! To
preserve and renew our relish for them, is not the veil of night
alternately drawn over her face, and doth she not change her
dress with the seasons?

George Berkeley, 'Three Dialogues between Hylas and Philonous'

Still south I went and west and south again,
Through Wicklow from the morning till the night,
And far from cities, and the sights of men,
Lived with the sunshine, and the moon's delight.

I knew the stars, the flowers, and the birds,
The grey and wintry sides of many glens,
And did but half remember human words,
In converse with the mountains, moors, and fens.

J. M. Synge, 'Prelude'

I t is to the sad, the lonely, the insatiable, that Nature reveals her
mysteries.

George Townshend, THE GENIUS OF IRELAND

'Why do you like the evening tide?'
    'It's like walking into a picture,' she said.

Brendan Kennelly, 'Picture'

She hath a woven garland all of the sighing sedge,
    And all her flowers are snowdrops grown in the
        winter's edge;
    The golden looms of Tir na n'Og wove all the winter
        through
    Her gown of mist and raindrops shot with a cloudy
        blue.

Nora Hopper, 'April in Ireland'

Now sweetly lies old Ireland,
    Emerald green beyond the foam,
    Awakening sweet memories,
    Calling the heart back home.

An Irish blessing

God gave the country
        A flower, a bird,
    To comfort his children
        For the flaming sword.

For easing and pleasing
        He made a tree,
    Many a sweet rivulet,
        Dew, and the bee.

God made the country
        Man made the town.
    Is not God a Maker
        Of great renown?

Katherine Tynan, 'The Maker'

The skilled agricultural labourer who really knows his business is a being who employs his brains as much and draws upon as varied a field of knowledge as the average schoolmaster. It is true that his knowledge is not book knowledge, but a love of earth and sky, a gathering of experience and tradition, the harvest of an eye which has been familiar with country sounds and sights and the ritual and procession of the seasons for many years, and has gathered almost unconsciously in the time a knowledge so vast and varied that if a really clever townsman, a man clever enough, let us say to become a member of Parliament, were told to acquire all the knowledge of a skilled agricultural labourer, after five years of application he would still be an amateur in comparison with his master ... Our standards of human values are all wrong. The townsman calls the farmer Patty or Hodge, and the countryman is affected by this pert assumption of superiority, his children especially so, whereas the countryman presiding over the mysteries of growth, of birth, nutrition, breeding, plant life, would be quite justified by the intellectual character of his employment in regarding most city folk as the lapsed barbarians of nature, outcasts from the great mother, decaying in intelligence, health, beauty, dignity, and all that makes a man worthy of regard.

A. E., 'What is Manual Labour?' THE IRISH HOMESTEAD,
25 May 1912

How alien, how unworthy of an earth so lovely and so majestic are the cities which man, with such pride, has been building for himself! How dark, unwholesome, and how pitiful seem these elaborate and labyrinthian prisons in which man has chosen to manacle his spirit! As modernity grows more intense, more sophisticated, the cities that men rear grow further and further from all that is exquisite, glorious, and uplifting in Nature.

George Townshend, THE GENIUS OF IRELAND

nature is a marvellous sedative. How infinite her ingeniousness amidst all our pains and fears.

Edward Martyn, THE HEATHER FIELD

I arise to-day
Through the strength of heaven:
Light of sun,
Radiance of moon,
Splendour of fire,
Speed of lightning,
Swiftness of wind,
Depth of sea,
Stability of earth,
Firmness of rock.

Attributed to St Patrick, 'The Deer's Cry' (trans. Kuno Meyer)

I invoke the land of Ireland,
Shining, shining sea;
Fertile, fertile Mountain;
Gladed, gladed wood!
Abundant river, abundant in water!
Fish-abounding lake!

Attributed to Amergin [invocation to Ireland] (trans. T. W. Rolleston)

they're all gone now, and there isn't anything more the sea can do to me. … I'll have no call now to be up crying and praying when the wind breaks from the south, and you can hear the surf is in the east, and the surf is in the west, making a great stir with the two noises, and they hitting one on the other.

J. M. Synge, RIDERS TO THE SEA

[I REMEMBERED] spring in Ireland. ... Soft grey days came first with quiet clouds, and the woods grew purple with sap, while a few birches that stood out before them like candle-sticks with wrought silver stems covered themselves with a mist of red. Then the hazels came out and hung the woods with straight ear-rings of gold, till one morning after rain spectres of pale green and yellow and pink began to look out between the trees. Then everything stood waiting for a moment till warmth came in the beginning of May, and the whole country broke out into wonderful glory – infinitely timid greens and yellows and whites, and birds singing everywhere, and strange odours creeping up into my room.

J. M. Synge, 'Vita Vecchia'

my love to thee, O land in the east, and 'tis ill for me to leave thee, for delightful are thy coves and havens, thy kind soft flowery fields, thy pleasant green-sided hills, and little was our need for departing.

Anonymous, 'Deirdré's Farewell to Alba' (trans. George Sigerson)

> Awake thee, my Bessy, the morning is fair,
>   The breath of young roses is fresh on the air,
>   The sun has long glanced over mountain and lake,
>   Then awake from thy slumbers, my Bessy, awake.
>
> Oh come whilst the flowers are still wet with the dew,
>   I'll gather the fairest, my Bessy, for you,
>   The lark poureth forth his sweet strain for thy sake,
>   Then awake from thy slumbers, my Bessy, awake.
>
> The hare from her soft bed of heather hath gone,
>   The coote to the water already hath flown –
>   There is life on the mountain and joy on the lake,
>   Then awake from thy slumbers, my Bessy, awake.

Jeremiah Joseph Callanan, 'Song'

The country silence wraps me quite,
  Silence and song and pure delight;
  The country beckons all the day,
  Smiling, and but a step away.

Katherine Tynan, 'The Old Love'

Enchantment is a fact in nature.

Standish O'Grady, 'The Great Enchantment'

My hope, my love, we will go
  Into the woods, scattering the dews,
  Where we will behold the salmon, and the ousel in
    its nest,
  The deer and the roe-buck calling,
  The sweetest bird on the branches warbling,
  The cuckoo on the summit of the green hill;
  And death shall never approach us
  In the bosom of the fragrant wood!

Anonymous, 'My Hope, My Love' (trans. Edward Walsh)

The sailor tells the children
  His stories of the sea,
  Their eyes look over the water
  To where his wonders be.

Oliver St John Gogarty, 'Kingdoms'

To Erin alone is my memory given,
  To Meath and to Munster my wild thoughts flow,
  To the shores of Moy-linny, the slopes of Loch Leven,
  And the beautiful land the Ultonians know.

Attributed to St Columcille (trans. Douglas Hyde)

Is not the sea
　　Made for the free,
Land for courts and chains alone?
　　Here we are slaves,
　　But on the waves
Love and liberty's all our own!
No eye to watch, and no tongue to wound us,
All earth forgot, and all heaven around us! –
　　Then come o'er the sea,
　　Maiden! with me,
Come wherever the wild wind blows;
　　Seasons may roll,
　　But the true soul
Burns the same where'er it goes.

Thomas Moore, 'Come O'er the Sea'

Ah me! they say if I could stand
　　Upon those mountain ledges,
I should but see on either hand
　　Plain fields and dusty hedges;
And yet I know my fairy-land
　　Lies somewhere o'er their edges.

Cecil Frances Alexander, 'Dreams'

I dreamt a dream, a dazzling dream, of a green isle far
　　away,
　　Where the glowing west to the ocean's breast calleth
　　　the dying day;
　　And that island green was as fair a scene as ever
　　　man's eye did see,
　　With its chieftains bold, and its temples old, and its
　　　homes and its altars free!

D. F. MacCarthy, 'A Dream of the Future'

The winds are roaring out of the West
  Where the clouds are in stormy saffron drest,
  And the curlew and wild-geese are calling and crying
  Over the straits in Inisgallun,
  The heron and cormorant wailing and sighing,
  Mingling a wild and an endless tune.

The winds are roaring out of the West
  Over the waters of strife and unrest,
  The shrieking rain in the low pools falling,
  The strong waves beating a ceaseless rune,
  And the heron and curlew and wild-geese calling,
  Vainly lamenting in Inisgallun.

The froth and fume of the maddened sea
  Spit thro' the torn air ceaselessly;
  And the dark low bog in anguish crying,
  And the heather wailing in bitter pain;
  For the winds from out of the West are flying
  And the Earth will never find peace again.

Darrell Figgis, 'Inisgallun'

I am Ireland:
  I am older than the Old Woman of Beare.

Great my glory:
  I that bore Cuchulainn the valiant.

Great my shame:
  My own children that sold their mother.

I am Ireland:
  I am lonelier than the Old Woman of Beare.

Padraic Pearse, 'I Am Ireland'

I long to be in the heart of an island, on a rocky peak, to look out often upon the smooth surface of the sea.

To see the great waves on glittering ocean ceaselessly chanting music to their Father.

To watch without melancholy its smooth, bright-bordered strand, to hear the cry of wondrous birds – what pleasing sound!

To hear the murmur of little waves against the rocks, to listen to the sea-sound, like keening by a graveyard.

To watch across the watery sea its splendid bird-flocks, to behold – greater than any wonder – its monstrous whales.

To see the changing course of ebb and flood; and this to be my name – I tell a secret thing – "He who turned his back on Ireland".

Anonymous, Untitled (trans. Myles Dillon)

"What will you do, love, when I am going,
　With white sail flowing,
　　The seas beyond? –
What will you do, love, when waves divide us,
And friends may chide us
　For being fond?"
"Though waves divide us, and friends be chiding,
In faith abiding,
　I'll still be true!
And I'll pray for thee on the stormy ocean,
In deep devotion –
　That's what I'll do!"

Samuel Lover, 'What Will You Do, Love'

divine
life

GOD

I arise to-day
    Through God's strength to pilot me:
    God's might to uphold me,
    God's wisdom to guide me,
    God's eye to look before me,
    God's ear to hear me,
    God's word to speak for me,
    God's hand to guard me,
    God's way to lie before me,
    God's shield to protect me,
    God's host to save me
    From snares of devils,
    From temptations of vices,
    From every one who shall wish me ill,
    Afar and anear,
    Alone and in a multitude.

Attributed to St Patrick, 'The Deer's Cry' (trans. Kuno Meyer)

Who have come have gone, who shall come must go,
But the graces of God shall forever flow.

Anonymous, 'Who Came Have Gone' (trans. Douglas Hyde)

God's help is nearer than the door.

An Irish proverb

The object of every man's mortal life was to attain the purpose of creation: namely, the soul's communion with God.

George Townshend, THE GENIUS OF IRELAND

The love of God directs everything good.

An Irish proverb

Sure the world knows that a man is born with the gift, and isn't the gift then the sign of the grace of God?

Padraic Colum, THE FIDDLER'S HOUSE

Only a fool would fail
  To praise God in His might
  When the tiny mindless birds
  Praise Him in their flight.

Anonymous, 'God's Praises' (trans. Brendan Kennelly)

The Power Divine is on the earth:
  Give thanks to God before ye die!

Aubrey de Vere, 'The Year of Sorrow'

All things bright and beautiful,
  All creatures great and small,
All things wise and wonderful,
  The Lord God made them all ....

He gave us eyes to see them,
  And lips that we might tell
How great is God Almighty,
  Who has made all things well.

Cecil Frances Alexander, 'All Things Bright and Beautiful'

That man communion with his God might share
  Below, Christ gave the ordinance of prayer:
Vague ambages and witless ecstasies
Avail not: ere a voice to prayer be given,
The heart should rise on wings of love to heaven.

Aubrey de Vere, 'The Right Use of Prayer'

Look not, nor sigh, for earthly throne,
  Nor place thy trust in arm of clay:
    But on thy knees
Uplift thy soul to God alone,
  For all things go their destined way,
    As He decrees.

*James Clarence Mangan, 'Lament for the Princes of Tir-Owen and
Tirconnell' (trans. by the author)*

God is perfect in knowledge; his understanding is infinite. He is the Father of lights. He looketh to the ends of the earth, and seeth under the whole heaven.

George Berkeley, 'The Christian Idea of God'

I rise up with God,
    May God rise up with me,
    God's hand round about me,
    Sitting and lying,
    And rising of me.

Anonymous, 'I Rise Up' (trans. Douglas Hyde)

The will of God be done by us.
    The law of God be kept by us,
    Our evil will controlled by us,
    Our tongue in check be held by us,
    Repentance timely made by us,
    Christ's passion understood by us,
    Each sinful crime be shunned by us,
    Much on the *End* be mused by us,
    And Death be blessed found by us,
    With Angels' music heard by us,
    And God's high praise sung to us,
    For ever and for aye.

Anonymous, 'Blessed Be the Holy Will of God' (trans. Douglas Hyde)

Thus spake a man in days of old:
    I will believe that God can be
    The kind, the just, that we are told,
    If He will throw down here to me
    A bag of gold –

But when his wife rose from her bed
    To see what kept her man away,
    She found him, with a broken head:
    And on the ground beside him lay
    … A bag of lead!

James Stephens, 'Irony'

Be Thou my vision, O Lord of my heart,
  Naught is all else to me, save that Thou art.

Thou my best thought by day and by night,
  Waking or sleeping, Thy presence my light.

Be Thou my wisdom, Thou my true word;
  I ever with Thee, Thou with me, Lord.

Anonymous, 'A Prayer' (trans. Eleanor Hull)

'O King, who art in heaven ... I scream to Thee again and again aloud, For it is Thy grace I am hoping for.

'I am in age, and my shape is withered; many a day I have been going astray ... When I was young, my deeds were evil; I delighted greatly in quarreling and rows. I liked much better to be playing or drinking on a Sunday morning than to be going to Mass ... I was given to great oaths, and I did not let lust or drunkenness pass me by ... The day has stolen away, and I have not raised the hedge until the crop in which Thou didst take delight is destroyed ... I am a worthless stake in a corner of a hedge, or I am like a boat that has lost its rudder, that would be broken against a rock in the sea, and that would be drowned in the cold waves.'

Raftery, 'Repentance' (trans. Lady Gregory)

If one must offer any prayer
  to much-beleaguered heaven –
  preserve your sense of humour, be merciful and fair,
  for only God's wild laughter
  could hope that things will turn out even.

Brendan Kennelly, 'A Special Odour'

Righteousness, piety and the holy

Think not what you are, wretched man, but what you will be ... Do not be sure about things that perish and unsure about the better things that shall last ... Awake, my sons, from darkness, seek the light, that you may both see and be seen ... Sleep not, lest you believe the false to be the true ... Life is a wheel, it runneth today and waiteth not for thee, who should run with it ... Sell not your inheritance in heaven; sell your faults, above all, your pride, and buy virtues, buy humility ... He tramples on the world who tramples on himself ... He who loves has accomplished all and never grows old and feeble ... Perchance by aid of love we shall escape the penalty of our folly in this world, of our ignorance of the things that really matter. So give of your charity to those who need ... Do not prize your wealth before yourself, your possessions above your soul. For what is really yours except your soul? Truly patience for one hour is better than penitence throughout eternity.

St Columbanus, from 'Sermons' (trans. Eleanor Shipley Duckett)

Cease to do evil – learn to do well.

Biblical inscription on Richmond Penitentiary, Dublin

A man's very highest moment is, I have no doubt at all, when he kneels in the dust, and beats his breast, and tells all the sins of his life.

Oscar Wilde, letter to Alfred Douglas, 1897

I believe every individual to be the architect of his own happiness or misery.

James Clarence Mangan, AUTOBIOGRAPHY

Sin or moral turpitude doth not consist in the outward physical action or motion, but in the internal deviation of the will from the laws of reason and religion.

George Berkeley, 'Three Dialogues between Hylas and Philonous'

> Good luck to you, don't scorn the poor, and don't be
> their despiser,
> For worldly wealth soon melts away, and cheats the
> very miser,
> And Death soon strips the proudest wreath from
> haughty human brows;
> Then don't be stiff, and don't be proud, good
> Woman of Three Cows!

Anonymous, 'The Woman of Three Cows' (trans. James Clarence Mangan)

the highest form of genius is the genius for sanctity, the genius for noble life and thought.

Padraic Pearse, 'The Spiritual Nation'

Many men for me have sued,
    Sought in court, in secret woo'd,
    Never one have I come nigh
    For my path lay pure and high.

Anonymous, 'Fand's Farewell to Cuchulainn' (trans. George Sigerson)

What can it profit my race if it gain the empire of the world and yet lose its own soul – a soul which is only now growing to self-consciousness.

A. E., 'Nationality and Imperialism'

May thy holy angels, O Christ, son of the living God,
    tend our sleep, our rest, our bright bed.

Let them reveal true visions to us in our sleep, O High-
    prince of the universe, O great mysterious King.

May no demons, no ill, no injury or terrifying dreams
    disturb our rest, our prompt and swift repose.

May our waking, our work and our activity be holy; our
    sleep, our rest, unhindered and untroubled.

Attributed to St Patrick, 'Evening Hymn' (trans. Gerard Murphy)

I thank God that my middle place
    Is set amid such pleasantness,

And not too high and not too low
    The safe, untroubled path I go.

Katherine Tynan, 'Thanksgiving'

The contemplative life, the life that has for its aim not *doing* but *being*, and not *being* merely, but *becoming* – that is what the critical spirit can give us.

Oscar Wilde, 'The Critic as Artist'

May the road rise with you,
    May the wind be always at your back,
    May the sun shine warm upon your face,
    And the rains fall soft upon your fields,
    And, until we meet again
    May God keep you in the hollow of his hand.

An Irish blessing

Holy Spirit, to win
    Body and soul within,
    To guide us that we be
    From ills and illness free,

From sin and demons' snare,
    From Hell and evils there,
    O Holy Spirit, come!
    Hallow our heart, Thy home.

Maelisu, 'Holy Spirit' (George Sigerson)

And be the judge of your own soul; but never for a second, I implore you, set up as the judge of another. Commentator, annotator, if you like, but never judge.

Kate O'Brien, THE LAND OF SPICES

I kindle this little light,
    on the Earth plane.
    I dedicate it to the
    service of the Spirit.
    I guard and cherish
    this light as a living symbol,
    and an act of Faith in the
    Reality of the powers of Light.

'The Invocation of Light', a Celtic prayer

christian tradition

I arise to-day
    Through the strength of the love of Cherubim,
    In obedience of angels,
    In the service of archangels,
    In hope of resurrection to meet with reward,
    In prayers of patriarchs,
    In predictions of prophets,
    In preachings of apostles,
    In faiths of confessors,
    In innocence of holy virgins,
    In deeds of righteous men.

Attributed to St Patrick, 'The Deer's Cry' (trans. Kuno Meyer)

Thou art my king. Thou art my law. My flesh, my body are thine. I love thee, blessed Christ, for my soul is thine tonight.

Airbertach mac Cosse Dobráin, 'I Invoke Thee, God'
(trans. Gerard Murphy)

Pilgrim, take care your journey's not in vain,
    a hazard without profit, without gain;
    the King you seek you'll find in Rome, it's true,
    but only if he travels on the way with you.

Anonymous, 'Pilgrimage To Rome' (trans. James Carney)

here for you from heaven is a gleaming row of gorgeous gems, the fruitful teachings of God to us; copious showers cast forth by Scripture. We have not given them, that is no loss, a tempering in lustrous Gaelic; in God, in the lake-spring of jewels, what immersion have they not had? I did not, it was not for me to do, darken with brilliance of words the glistening gem-tempered throng from heaven, the lustrous words of our Creator.

Giolla Brighde, poem prefixed to 'Christian Doctrine' (trans. Eleanor Knott)

Thanks be to Christ for all things,
    Protect me, Friend, do not betray us, King of Kings,
    Oh Lord of Heaven who bought us dearly
    From the fetters of worldly sin relieve us,
    Withhold your anger, give us strength to live,
    Save our souls.

Donncha Rua Mac Conmara, 'The Adventures of a Miserable Wretch
to this Point' (trans. Joan Keefe)

Think of Tone ... how as he worked among them he grew to know and love the real, the historic Irish people, and the great, clear, sane conception came to him that in Ireland there must be not two nations or three nations but one nation, that Protestant and Dissenter must be brought into amity with Catholic and that Catholic, Protestant and Dissenter must unite to achieve freedom for all.

Padraic Pearse, address delivered at the grave of Wolfe Tone

O Jesus Christ, O light of graces,
  Ruling in heaven and earthly places,
  Who pourest thy blood on the tree to save me
  From Death and the Devil who would enslave me.

Alas! how badly did I requite thee!
  Ready was I to hurt, to smite thee,
  To open thy wounds by unbelieving,
  Forgetting that all things are of thy giving.

What profit me now – my case is piteous –
  All friends, companions, worldly riches;
  For Death is upon me with a warrant written,
  Oh! pardon! pardon! or I am smitten.

Anonymous, 'The Man Before Death' (trans. Douglas Hyde)

These last words of mine I commend to you, O little children, that ye preserve a mutual charity with peace, and a charity not feigned amongst yourselves; and if ye observe to do this according to the example of the holy fathers, God, the comforter of the good, shall help you, and I, remaining with Him, shall make intercession for you, and not only the necessaries of this present life shall be sufficiently supplied you by Him, but also the reward of eternal good, prepared for the observers of things Divine, shall be rendered you.

Attributed to St Columcille (trans. Douglas Hyde)

Every good gift is of God; all power is of God; and He who has given the power, and from Whom alone it originates, will never suffer the exercise of it to be practised upon any less solid foundation than the power itself.

Edmund Burke, 'Speeches on the Impeachment of Warren Hastings,
15 February 1788'

Christianity is a personal thing given into every man's own keeping, whereby he may save his own soul or lose it.

George Moore, Salve

> Mary, splendid diadem, Thou that hast saved our race,
>   Glorious noble torch, orchard of Kings!
>
> Brilliant one, transplendent one, with the deed of pure chastity,
>   Fair golden illumined ark, holy daughter from Heaven!
>
> Mother of righteousness, Thou that excellest all else,
>   Pray with me Thy first-born to save me on the day of Doom.
>
> Noble rare star, tree under blossom,
>   Powerful choice lamp, sun that warmeth every one.

Anonymous, 'A Prayer to the Virgin' (trans. Kuno Meyer)

The paradise of the Christian, as those who think more of the order of communities than of the nature of things have shaped it, is but the fulfilment of one dream; but the paradise that the common people tell of about the fire, and still half understand, is the fulfilment of all dreams, and opens its gates as gladly to the perfect lover as to the perfect saint, and only he who understands it can lift romance into prophecy and make beauty holy.

W. B. Yeats, 'The Literary Movement in Ireland'

I am repentant, Lord, for my transgression, as is right: Christ, of thy mercy, forgive me every sin that may be attributed to me.

Óengus céile Dé, 'Prayer for Forgiveness' (trans. Gerard Murphy)

God be with me against all trouble, noble Trinity which
is one, Father, Son, and Holy Spirit.

The bright holy King of the sun, who is more beautiful
than anything to which we have a right, is a
wondrous refuge for me against the host of black
demons.

The Father, the Son, the glorious Holy Spirit, may these
three protect me against all plague-bearing clouds.

Anonymous, 'God Be With Me' (trans. Gerard Murphy)

I am Eve, great Adam's wife,
    because of me has Jesus died;
    it were I, thief of my children's heaven,
    by all rights were crucified.

I had a king's house to my wish,
    but made an evil choice one day
    that withered both my flesh and soul
    and left my hand unclean this way.

Anonymous, 'Eve' (trans. James Carney)

Let us rest,
    from the weight of the world's weariness;
    let us be young,
    to whom sorrow is not decreed
    forever,
    for whom our portion is not tragedy
    without end,
    nor our lot bondage
    by virtue of the victory of Christ,
    who is gentle.

Gearóid Ó Clérigh, 'Prayer' (trans. by the author)

faith and spirituality

f aith arouses intuition or spiritual insight, and by this power man bursts the bounds of his hell and escapes for ever from the limitations of corporeal blindness.

George Townshend, The Genius of Ireland

To imitate the sun
   is to let the light become
   dream-architect, image-maker
   working in the dark to shape
   maps tracing the spirit's journey
   forward to its beginnings
   of infinite simplicity.

Brendan Kennelly, 'To imitate the sun'

Y ou will find your real faith in the hour of trial.

George Bernard Shaw, Androcles and the Lion

It may even be that a World-soul is personally conscious of all its past, and that individual souls, as they enter into deeper consciousness enter into something which is at once reminiscence and actuality.

Myers as quoted by Lady Gregory in 'Seers and Healers'

Those who see any difference between soul and body have neither.

Oscar Wilde, 'Phrases and Philosophies for the use of the Young'

As sure therefore as the sensible world really exists, so sure is there an infinite omnipresent spirit who contains and supports it.

George Berkeley, 'Three Dialogues between Hylas and Philonous'

It will be known from this that God is able
   To help the fainting, to lift up the poor.
Even in the barren place to set a table
   His help, though slow in coming, cometh sure.

For He, whose voice is in the crashing thunder
   Whose breath gives lightning and the storm-wind
      birth,
Works in our sight each year as great a wonder
   Calling up harvests from the silent earth.

Happy are we, such miracle discerning,
   And happy those, in quiet later days
Who, of the marvels of the old time learning,
   Will know that God may work in many ways!

Lady Gregory, COLMAN AND GUAIRE

But a great deal of *Free-thinking* will at last set us all right, and every one will adhere to the *Scripture* he likes best; by which means Religion, Peace, and Wealth, will be for ever secured in Her Majesty's Realms.

Jonathan Swift, 'Mr. Collins's Discourse of Free-Thinking'

We can learn to know a man's mind, but we can rarely be quite sure that we know his soul. That is a book which only God reads plainly.

Padraic Pearse, 'The Spiritual Nation'

But well for him whose feet have trod
    The weary road of earthly strife
    Yet from the sorrows of his life
Builds ladders to be nearer God.

Oscar Wilde, 'Cry Woe, Woe, and Let the Good Prevail'

But I do say that when people have happiness within themselves, all the earthquakes, all the floods, and all the prisons in the world can't make them really unhappy. ... I say that if you've happiness within yourself, you don't need to seek it outside, spending money on drink and theatres and bad company, and being miserable after all. You can sit at home and be happy; and you can work and be happy. If you have that in you, the spirit will set you free to do what you want and guide you to do right. But if you haven't got it, then you'd best be respectable and stick to the ways that are marked out for you; for you've nothing else to keep you straight.

George Bernard Shaw, FANNY'S FIRST PLAY

I do not think that there can be any education of which spiritual religion does not form an integral part; as it is the most important part of life, so it should be the most important part of education, which some have defined as a preparation for complete life.

Padraic Pearse, 'The Murder Machine'

We have just enough religion to make us hate, but not enough to make us love one another.

Jonathan Swift, 'Thoughts on Various Subjects'

Let us for once turn our eyes on those things in which we have one common interest. Why should disputes about faith interrupt the duties of civil life, or the different roads we take to heaven prevent our taking the same steps on earth?

George Berkeley, 'A Word to the Wise'

In the name of the Father full of virtue,
   in the name of the Son Who suffered pain,
   in the name of the Holy Ghost in power,
   Mary and her Son be with us. ...

Likewise it shall be done to you:
   all good things shall first be yours.
Heaven is your inheritance.
   Be not faint-hearted in your faith.

Fear Dorcha Ó Mealláin, 'Exodus to Connacht'
(trans. Thomas Kinsella)

saints and scholars

to consider that this great gift of spiritual sensibility belongs in a marked degree to the Irish: to look back on a distant past and see how the religious genius of the people made this lovely island once the shrine of Western Europe: to realise that still there burns deep in the dumb heart of the people that ancient fire: to hear to-day in our midst the voice of poets beginning to raise again the strain so long unheard, and chant in the ears of a forgetful world the praise of eternal beauty and eternal truth: thus to watch, to listen, and to reflect is to be filled with hope that Ireland may not be slow to catch the vision of a breaking day, or to hear the tidings already breathed from on high, and that she may do for mankind now such service as her saints and scholars did for Europe long ago.

George Townshend, THE GENIUS OF IRELAND

For we are the disciples of SS. Peter and Paul and of all the disciples who by inspiration of the Holy Spirit wrote the divine canon; we, all the Irish, dwellers at the ends of the earth, have never accepted anything but the evangelical and apostolic teaching. No one of us has been a heretic, no one a Jew, no one a schismatic, but the Catholic faith, just as it was first transmitted by you, to wit, the successors of the holy apostles, is maintained unchanged. For we are bound to the Chair of Peter; although Rome is great and famous, through that Chair only is it great and famous with us.

St Columbanus, letter to Pope Boniface IV

The Saviour told Patrick one time to go and prepare a man that was going to die. And Patrick said "I would sooner not go for I never yet saw the soul part from the body." But after that he went and prepared the man. And when he was lying there dead, he saw the soul go from the body, and three times it went to the door and three times it came back and kissed the body. And Patrick asked the Saviour why it did that and he said "That soul was sorry to part from the body because it had kept it so clean and so honest."

Lady Gregory, A BOOK OF SAINTS AND WONDERS

"Lon is dead (Lon is dead);
    To Cill Garad it is a great misfortune;
    To Eirinn with its countless tribes;
    It is a destruction of learning and of schools.

"Lon has died (Lon has died);
    In Cill Garad great the misfortune;
    It is a destruction of learning and of schools,
    To the Island of Eirinn beyond her boundaries."

Eulogy in honor of Longarad the Scholar as quoted by Seumas MacManus

These were the wishes of Brigit:

> "I would wish a great lake of ale for the King of
> Kings; I would wish the family of Heaven to be
> drinking it through life and time.
> "I would wish the men of Heaven in my own house;
> I would wish vessels of peace to be giving to them.
> "I would wish vessels full of alms to be giving away; I
> would wish ridges of mercy for peace-making.
> "I would wish joy to be in their drinking; I would
> wish Jesus to be here among them.
> "I would wish the three Marys of great name; I
> would wish the people of Heaven from every side.
> "I would wish to be a rent-payer to the Prince; the
> way if I was in trouble he would give me a good
> blessing."
> Whatever, now, Brigit would ask of the Lord, he
> would give it to her on the moment. And it is
> what her desire was, to satisfy the poor, to banish
> every hardship, and to save every sorrowful man.

Lady Gregory, A BOOK OF SAINTS AND WONDERS

I read or write, I teach or wonder what is truth,
  I call upon my God by night and day.
  I eat and freely drink, I make my rhymes,
  And snoring sleep, or vigil keep and pray.
  And very ware of all my shames am I;
  O Mary, Christ, have mercy on your man!

Sedulius Scottus ['The Christian Virgil'] as quoted by Francis Carty

O Cormac, beautiful is thy church,
  With its books and learning
  A devout city with a hundred crosses.

Cross inscription addressed to an abbot of Durrow

art and literature

the BARÒIC tRAÒITION

The bardic literature of Erin stands alone, as distinctively and genuinely Irish as the race itself, or the natural aspects of the island.

Standish O'Grady, EARLY BARDIC LITERATURE

Literature is, to my mind, the great teaching power of the world, the ultimate creator of all values, and it is this, not only in the sacred books whose power everybody acknowledges, but by every movement of imagination in song or story or drama that height of intensity and sincerity has made literature at all. Literature must take the responsibility of its power, and keep all its freedom: it must be like the spirit and like the wind that blows where it listeth; it must claim its right to pierce through every crevice of human nature, and to describe the relation of the soul and the heart to the facts of life and of law, and to describe that relation as it is, not as we would have it be; and in so far as it fails to do this it fails to give us that foundation of understanding and charity for whose lack our moral sense can be but cruelty.

W. B. Yeats, 'Samhain: 1903'

A nation is hidden behind its literature. The writings of a people form a mirror in which the popular mind and heart are reflected. A poet is not a creator only, but a revealer; and he reveals, not only his own soul, but the soul of his people and of his age.

George Townshend, THE GENIUS OF IRELAND

The following ancient rann contains the four
  qualifications of a bard:
      Purity of hand, bright, without wounding,
      Purity of mouth, without poisonous satire,
      Purity of learning, without reproach,
      Purity, as a husband, in wedlock.

Ancient bardic rann (trans. Standish O'Grady)

The word 'poet' is here apparently equivalent to druid, as the word 'druid' like the Latin *vates* is frequently a synonym for 'poet'.

Douglas Hyde, A LITERARY HISTORY OF IRELAND

The *filé* [poet] is the Word of Science, he is the god who gives to man the fire of thought; and as science is not distinct from its object, as God and Nature are but one, the being of the *filé* is mingled with the winds and the waves, with the wild animals and the warrior's arms.

Henri d'Arbois de Jubainville, as quoted by T. W. Rolleston,
MYTHS AND LEGENDS OF THE CELTIC RACE

The word is energy, it kept me going. When it stops, everything stops. Today's world is all images, no words.

Samuel Beckett, conversation with the editor

We are the music makers
And we are the dreamers of dreams,
Wandering by lone sea-breakers,
And sitting by desolate streams; –
World-losers and world-forsakers,
On whom the pale moon gleams:
Yet we are the movers and shakers
Of the world for ever, it seems.

With wonderful deathless ditties
We build up the world's great cities,
And out of a fabulous story
We fashion an empire's glory:
One man with a dream, at pleasure,
Shall go forth and conquer a crown;
And three with a new song's measure
Can trample an empire down.

We, in the ages lying
In the buried past of the earth
Built Nineveh with our sighing,
And Babel itself with our mirth;
And o'erthrew them with prophesying,
To the old of the new world's worth;
For each age is a dream that is dying,
Or one that is coming to birth

Arthur O'Shaughnessy, 'Ode'

There are two conceptions of poetry. ... The first regards the poet as a seer and a spiritual force; the second as an aristocratic craftsman. The first looks to man himself as the source of inspiration; the second to tradition, to the forms and images in which old conceptions have been embodied – old faiths, myths, dreams.

John Eglinton, 'National Drama and Contemporary Life'

His songs were a little phrase
    Of eternal song,
  Drowned in the harping of lays
    More loud and long.

His deed was a single word,
    Called out alone
  In a night when no echo stirred
    To laughter or moan.

But his songs new souls shall thrill,
    The loud harps dumb,
  And his deed the echoes fill
    When the dawn is come.

Thomas MacDonagh, 'Of a Poet Patriot'

And thou, sweet Poetry, thou loveliest maid …
  Thou source of all my bliss, and all my woe,
  That found'st me poor at first, and keep'st me so;
  Thou guide by which the nobler arts excel,
  Thou nurse of every virtue fare thee well! …
  Still let thy voice, prevailing over time,
  Redress the rigours of the inclement clime;
  Aid slighted truth with thy persuasive strain;
  Teach erring man to spurn the rage of gain:
  Teach him, that states of native strength possest,
  Though very poor, may still be very blest.

Oliver Goldsmith, 'The Deserted Village'

What is an Irish poet who has lost his idealism? He is as a saint without the knowledge of heaven, as a scholar without the knowledge of the earth.

George Townshend, THE GENIUS OF IRELAND

'Tis the old, old story: one man will read
    His lesson of toil in the sky;
While another is blind to the present need.
    But sees with the spirit's eye.
You may grind their souls in the selfsame mill,
    You may bind them heart and brow;
But the poet will follow the rainbow still,
    And his brother will follow the plow.

John Boyle O'Reilly, 'The Rainbow's Treasure'

Pure poetry springs from a creative impulse of the poet's imagination pressing for definition. It is a spirit; one cannot bid it come. It expresses something beyond itself; something infinite that can satisfy not only the imagination but the whole of us. In true poetry sound and meaning are one; you experience the one in the other, and without the music to carry the meaning it is only prose.

Lord Dunsany as quoted by Hazel Littlefield

More lasting is Fame than the life of men,
    For tradition then may keep it young,
But more lasting still is the poet's pen,
    And the book that speaks with undying tongue.

Anonymous, 'More Lasting' (trans. Douglas Hyde)

You make beautiful poetry out of what you call your unhappiness' Maud Gonne told W. B. Yeats, 'and you are happy in that. Marriage would be such a dull affair. Poets should never marry. The world should thank me for not marrying you.'

Maud Gonne, A Servant of the Queen

The facts of life with which poetry is concerned are not the complex and conventional facts, but the simple and universal.

John Eglinton, 'Mr. Yeats and Popular Poetry'

A man is born solitary and dies solitary. Only the poet *lives* solitary.

John Butler Yeats, letter to W. B. Yeats, 8 December 1917

When the itch of literature comes over a man, nothing can cure it but the scratching of a pen.

Samuel Lover, HANDY ANDY

> I am Raftery the poet,
> Full of hope and love,
> With eyes that have no light,
> With gentleness that has no misery.
>
> Going west upon my pilgrimage
> By the light of my heart,
> Feeble and tired
> To the end of my road.
>
> Behold me now,
> And my face to a wall,
> A-playing music
> unto empty pockets.

Raftery, 'I am Raftery' (Douglas Hyde)

Art is a language, and it consists of physical signs.

William Larminie, 'Legends as Material for Literature'

Literature, to the common Irishman, is an ingenious collection of fine words which no doubt have some meaning, but which he is not going to presume to understand.

D. P. Moran, 'The Battle of Two Civilizations'

The centre of the national life is still among the poor and the workers, they alone have been true to Ireland, they alone are worthy and they alone are capable of fostering a national literature and a national dream.

Maud Gonne, The United Irishman, 24 October 1904

Roll forth, my song, like the rushing river,
That sweeps along to the mighty sea;
God will inspire me while I deliver
My soul of thee!

James Clarence Mangan, 'The Nameless One'

In all ages poets and thinkers have owed far less to their countries than their countries have owed to them.

John Eglinton, 'What Should be the Subjects of a National Drama?'

That is what all poets do: they talk to themselves out loud; and the world overhears them.

George Bernard Shaw, Candida

In old days books were written by men of letters and read by the public. Nowadays books are written by the public and read by nobody.

Oscar Wilde, 'A Few Maxims for the Instruction of the Over-Educated'

ow I claim for Irish literature at its best these excellences: a clearer than Greek vision, a more generous than Greek humanity, a deeper than Greek spirituality. And I claim that Irish literature has never lost those excellences: that they are of the essence of Irish nature and are characteristic of modern Irish folk poetry even as they are of ancient Irish epic and of mediaeval Irish hymns.

Padraic Pearse, 'Some Aspects of Irish Literature'

The horse of poetry nibbles
   The summer-riddled grass,
   Lifting his heavy head
   To the young girls as they pass;

Riderless he may drowse
   Till the year turn over.
   Leap girl upon his back
   And he will race for ever.

Donagh MacDonagh, 'The Invitation'

id the bards drop in song the seed of heroic virtues, and beget the mystic chivalry of the past, and flood our being with spiritual longings, that we might at last sink to clay and seek only to inherit the earth?

A. E., 'Nationality and Imperialism'

o all great nations their history presents itself under the aspect of poetry; a drama exciting pity and terror; an epic with unbroken continuity, and a wide range of thought, when the intellect is satisfied with coherence and unity, and the imagination by extent and diversity. Such is the bardic history of Ireland.

Standish O'Grady, EARLY BARDIC LITERATURE

Every life is a symphony, and the translation of this life into music, and from music back to literature or sculpture or painting is the real effort of the artist.

J. M. Synge, 'Autobiography'

You will admit that a man of weak intellect cannot write a fine style.

George Moore, SALVE

And I would have all know that when all falls
    In ruin, poetry calls out in joy,
    Being the scattering hand, the bursting pod,
    The victim's joy among the holy flame,
    God's laughter at the shattering of the world.

W. B. Yeats, THE KING'S THRESHOLD

The work is finished. I am both happy and sad. It is a strange feeling. Others discover in my writing a secret of which I am unaware. It is a secret which is hidden from me. Many people come to see me, and I am the only one who does not know why.

Samuel Beckett, conversation with the editor

myth and legend

And once Patrick asked [Keelta] how it was that the Fianna became so mighty and so glorious that all Ireland sang of their deeds, as Ireland has done ever since. Keelta answered: 'Truth was in our hearts and strength in our arms, and what we said, that we fulfilled.'

T. W. Rolleston, MYTHS AND LEGENDS OF THE CELTIC RACE

Adieu, sweet Angus, Maeve and Fand,
    Ye plumed yet skinny Shee,
    That poets played with hand in hand
    To learn their ecstasy.

We'll search in Red Dan Sally's ditch,
    And drink in Tubber fair,
    Or poach with Red Dan Philly's bitch
    The badger and the hare.

J. M. Synge, 'The Passing of the Shee'

I f we live influenced by wind and sun and tree, and not by the passions and deeds of the past we are a thriftless and a hopeless people.

From a knowledge of local history comes that permanent and proud nationality which appears to sacrifice life and wealth to liberty, but really wins all together.

Thomas Davis as quoted by Frank Gallagher in 'Davis and the Modern Revolution'

When the poet Amergin set foot upon the soil of Ireland it is said that he chanted a strange and mystical lay:

"I am the Wind that blows over the sea,
I am the Wave of the Ocean;
I am the Murmur of the billows;
I am the Ox of the Seven Combats;
I am the Vulture upon the rock;
I am a Ray of the Sun;
I am the fairest of Plants;
I am a Wild Boar in valour;
I am a Salmon in the Water;
I am a Lake in the plain;
I am the Craft of the artificer;
I am a Word of Science;
I am the Spear-point that gives battle;
I am the god that creates in the head of man the fire of thought.
Who is it that enlightens the assembly upon the mountain, if not I?
Who telleth the ages of the moon, if not I?
Who showeth the place where the sun goes to rest, if not I?"

Amergin the Poet (trans. T. W. Rolleston)

Royal and saintly Cashel! I would gaze
　　Upon the wreck of thy departed powers ...
　　There breathes from thy lone courts and voiceless
　　　aisles
　A melancholy moral; such as sinks
　　On the lone traveler's heart, amid the piles
　Of vast Persepolis on her mountain stand,
　Or Thebes half buried in the desert sand.

Aubrey de Vere, 'The Rock of Cashel'

The Druids ... refrained from committing their mysteries to writing, for writing is the source of heresies and confusions, and it was not well that the folk should discuss Divine things among themselves; for them the arts of war and the chase, and for the Druids meditation on eternal things. But there is no doubt that the Druids were well instructed in the heavens; and the orientation of the stones that surround their temples implies elaborate calculations.

George Moore, Salve

And they had a well below the sea where the nine hazels of wisdom were growing; that is, the hazels of inspiration and of the knowledge of poetry. And their leaves and their blossoms would break out in the same hour, and would fall on the well in a shower that raised a purple wave. And then the five salmon that were waiting there would eat the nuts, and their colour would come out in the red spots of their skin, and any person that would eat one of those salmon would know all wisdom and all poetry. And there were seven streams of wisdom that sprang from that well and turned back to it again; and the people of many arts have all drank from that well.

Lady Gregory, Gods and Fighting Men

O ur legends are always associated with places, and not merely every mountain and valley, but every strange stone and little coppice has its legend, preserved in written or unwritten tradition.

W. B. Yeats, 'A Note on National Drama'

Within our magic halls of brightness
　Trips many a foot of snowy whiteness, –
　Stolen maidens, queens of fairy,
　And kings and chiefs a slaugh shee airy.
　　Shuheen, sho, lulo lo!

Edward Walsh, 'The Fairy Nurse'

A fter they had kissed their daughter, the king took my hand, and said aloud in the hearing of the host –

"This is Oisin, the son of Finn, for whom my daughter, Niam, travelled over the sea to Erin. This is Oisin, who is to be the husband of Niam of the Golden Hair. We give you a hundred thousand welcomes, brave Oisin. You will be for ever young in this land. All kinds of delights and innocent pleasures are awaiting you, and my daughter, the gentle, golden-haired Niam, shall be your wife; for I am the king of Tirnanoge."

I gave thanks to the king, and I bowed low to the queen; after which we went into the palace, where we found a banquet prepared. The feasting and rejoicing lasted for ten days, and on the last day, I was wedded to the gentle Niam of the Golden Hair.

P. W. Joyce, OLD CELTIC ROMANCES

T he folk-tales of Connaught have ever lain nearer to the hearts of the people than those of Galilee. Whatever there is of worth in Celtic song and story is woven into them, imagery handed down from the dim Druidic ages.

George Moore, SALVE

"God forbid," said Keelta, "that I should take upon me a shape of sorcery, or any other than that which my Maker, the true and glorious God, hath bestowed upon me." And the Fairy Folk said: "It is the word of a true warrior and hero, and the thing that thou sayest is good." So they healed his wounds, and every bodily evil that he had, and he wished them blessing and victory, and went his way.

T. W. Rolleston, MYTHS AND LEGENDS OF THE CELTIC RACE

A land of youth, a land of rest,
    A land from sorrow free;
It lies far off in the golden west,
    On the verge of the azure sea.
A swift canoe of crystal bright,
    That never met mortal view –
We shall reach the land ere fall of night,
    In that strong and swift canoe:
        We shall reach the strand
        Of that sunny land,
    From druids and demons free;
        The land of rest,
        In the golden west,
    On the verge of the azure sea!

P. W. Joyce, OLD CELTIC ROMANCES

When the Dagda got possession of the harp, the tale goes on, he played on it the 'three noble strains' which every great master of the harp should command, namely, the Strain of Lament, which caused the hearers to weep, the Strain of Laughter, which made them merry, and the Strain of Slumber, or Lullaby, which plunged them all in a profound sleep. And under cover of that sleep the Danaan champion stole out and escaped.

T. W. Rolleston, MYTHS AND LEGENDS OF THE CELTIC RACE

O! blame me not if I love to dwell
     On Erin's early glory;
Oh! blame me not if too oft I tell
     The same inspiring story.
For sure 'tis much to know and feel
That the race now rated lowly
Once ruled as lords, with sceptre of steel;
     While our Island was yet the Holy.

Thomas D'Arcy McGee, 'Oh! blame me not'

m yth and history, dreams and facts, are forever inextricably commingled.

Sean O'Faolain, THE IRISH: A CHARACTER STUDY

By this magical wand,
     By the wizard's command,
I appoint and decree,
For Dermat and thee,
The same bitter strife,
The same span of life:
In the pride of his strength,
Thou shalt slay him at length:
Lo, Dermat O'Dyna
     Lies stretched in his gore;
Behold my avengers,
     The tusks of the boar!
And thus is decreed,
For Donn's cruel deed,
Sure vengeance to come –
His son's bloody doom;
By this wand in my hand,
By the wizard's command!

P. W. Joyce, OLD CELTIC ROMANCES

We must recreate and perpetuate in Ireland the knightly tradition of Cuchulain, the noble tradition of the Fianna, – 'We, the Fianna, never told a lie, falsehood was never imputed to us'; 'Strength in our hands, truth on our lips, cleanness in our hearts'; the Christ-like tradition of Columcille, 'if I should die it shall be from the excess of love I bear the Gael'.

Padraic Pearse, COLLECTED WORKS: POLITICAL WRITINGS AND SPEECHES *(1917)*

As quick as thought I grasped the elf,
    "Your fairy purse," I cried,
"My purse?" said he, " 'tis in her hand,
    That lady by your side."
I turned to look, the elf was off,
    And what was I to do?
Oh! I laughed to think what a fool I'd been,
    And, the fairy was laughing too.

Robert Dwyer Joyce, 'The Leprahaun'

A Leprecaun without a pot of gold is like a rose without perfume, a bird without a wing, or an inside without an outside.

James Stephens, THE CROCK OF GOLD

The seeds which are sown at the beginning of a race bear their flowers and fruits towards its close; and those antique names which already begin to stir us with their power, Angus, Lu, Deirdre, Finn, Ossian, and the rest, will be found to be each one the symbol of enduring qualities, and their story a trumpet through which will be blown the music of an eternal joy, the sentiment of an inexorable justice, the melting power of beauty in sorrow.

A. E., 'Nationality and Imperialism'

music and drama

It has often been remarked, and oftener felt, that our music is the truest of all comments upon our history. The tone of defiance, succeeded by the langour of despondency – a burst of turbulence dying away into softness – the sorrows of one moment lost in the levity of the next – and all that romantic mixture of mirth and sadness, which is naturally produced by the efforts of a lively temperament to shake off or forget the wrongs which lie upon it.

Thomas Moore, 'Prefatory Letter on Music'

I wish I were on yonder hill,
    For there I'd sit and cry my fill,
    Till every tear should turn a mill:
    Es go deh thu, mavourneen slaun.
    Shule, shule, shule agra!
    Only death can set me free,
    For the lad tha I loved is gone from me:
    Es go deh thu, mavourneen slaun.

'Shule Agra', an Irish song

Oh, give me one strain
Of that wild harp again …
And hearts, while they beat
To thy music so sweet,
Thy glories will ever prolong,
Land of honour and beauty and song!

Samuel Lover, 'Sweet Harp of the Days that are Gone'

music is the finest art, for it alone can express directly what is not utterable.

J. M. Synge, 'Étude Morbide'

In Dublin's fair city, where the girls are so pretty
I first set my eyes on sweet Molly Malone.
She wheel'd her wheelbarrow thro' streets broad and
narrow
Crying cockles and mussels! alive, alive, O!

She was a fishmonger, but sure 'twas no wonder,
For so were her father and mother before,
And they both wheel'd their barrow thro' streets
broad and narrow
Crying cockles and mussels! alive, alive, O!

She died of a fever, and none could relieve her,
And that was the end of sweet Molly Malone,
But her ghost wheels her barrow thro' streets broad
and narrow
Crying cockles and mussels! alive, alive, O!

'Molly Malone', an Irish song

the singer who lived is always alive: we hearken and always hear.

John Boyle O'Reilly, 'The Dead Singer'

a play to be suitable for performance at the Abbey should contain some criticism of life, founded on the experience or personal observation of the writer, or some vision of life, of Irish life by preference, important from its beauty or from some excellence of style; and this intellectual quality is not more necessary to tragedy than to the gayest comedy.

W. B. Yeats as quoted by Lady Gregory in OUR IRISH THEATRE

> The harp that once through Tara's halls
> The soul of music shed,
> Now hangs as mute on Tara's walls
> As if that soul were fled.
> So sleeps the pride of former days,
> So glory's thrill is o'er,
> And hearts that once beat high for praise,
> Now feel that pulse no more!
>
> No more to chiefs and ladies bright
> The harp of Tara swells;
> The chord alone that breaks at night,
> Its tale of ruin tells.
> Thus Freedom now so seldom wakes,
> The only throb she gives
> Is when some heart indignant breaks,
> To show that still she lives.

Thomas Moore, 'The Harp That Once Through Tara's Halls'

a play which pleases men and women of Ireland who have sold their country for ease and wealth, who fraternise with their country's oppressors or have taken service with them, a play that will please the host of English functionaries and the English garrison, is a play that can never claim to be a national literature.

Maud Gonne, THE UNITED IRISHMAN, *24 October 1904*

All art that is not conceived by a soul in harmony with some mood of the earth is without value, and unless we are able to produce a myth more beautiful than nature – holding in itself a spiritual grace beyond and through the earthly – it is better to be silent.

J. M. Synge, 'Étude Morbide'

Surely, if music ever spoke the misfortunes of a people, or could ever conciliate forgiveness for their errors, the music of Ireland ought to possess those powers.

Thomas Moore, 'Intolerance: A Satire'

We propose to have performed in Dublin, in the spring of every year certain Celtic and Irish plays, which whatever be their degree of excellence will be written with a high ambition, and so to build up a Celtic and Irish school of dramatic literature. We hope to find in Ireland an uncorrupted and imaginative audience trained to listen by its passion for oratory, and believe that our desire to bring upon the stage the deeper thoughts and emotions of Ireland will ensure for us a tolerant welcome, and that freedom to experiment which is not found in theatres of England, and without which no new movement in art or literature can succeed. We will show that Ireland is not the home of buffoonery and of easy sentiment, as it has been represented, but the home of an ancient idealism. We are confident of the support of all Irish people, who are weary of misrepresentation, in carrying out a work that is outside all the political questions that divide us.

Lady Gregory, OUR IRISH THEATRE

The drama is made serious … by the degree in which it gives the nourishment, not very easy to define, on which our imaginations live.

J. M. Synge, preface to THE TINKER'S WEDDING

We do not desire propagandist plays, nor plays written mainly to serve some obvious moral purpose; for art seldom concerns itself with those interests or opinions that can be defended by argument, but with realities of emotion and character that become self-evident when made vivid to the imagination.

W. B. Yeats as quoted by Lady Gregory in Our Irish Theatre

Love and reverence and the poetic imagination always effect such changes in the object of their passion. They are the essential condition of the transference of the real into the world of art.

Standish O'Grady, Early Bardic Literature

It is usually dangerous for anyone whose gift is one art to attempt to follow another, unless it so happens that he has more than one artistic gift.

Lord Dunsany, 'Three of the Arts' The Donnellan Lectures *1943*

Art, in a word, must not content itself simply with holding the mirror up to nature, for it is a re-creation more than a reflection, and not a repetition but rather a new song.

Oscar Wilde, 'Art at Willis's Rooms', Sunday Times,
25 December 1887

If the Arts should perish,
The world that lacked them would be like a woman
That, looking on the cloven lips of a hare,
Brings forth a hare-lipped child.

W. B. Yeats, The King's Threshold

eloquence and the power of utterance

Silence is preferable to mutilated statements.

Eamon de Valera, statement written from prison, December 1918

In the mean Time, I cannot but with some Pride, and much Pleasure, congratulate with my dear Country, which hath out-done all the Nations of *Europe*, in advancing the whole Art of Conversation, to the greatest Height it is capable of reaching.

Jonathan Swift, Introduction to 'Polite Conversation'

There is more power in speech than many people conceive. Thoughts come from God, they are born through the marriage of the head and the lungs. The head moulds the thought into the form of words, then it is borne and sounded on the air which has been already in the secret kingdoms of the body, which goes in bearing life and comes out freighted with wisdom.

James Stephens, THE CROCK OF GOLD

Say but little and say it well.

An Irish proverb

the Celts were always quick to take an artistic hint; they avoid the obvious and the commonplace; the half-said thing to them is dearest.

Kuno Meyer, ANCIENT IRISH POETRY

Utter not swaggering speech, nor say thou wilt not yield what is right; it is a shameful thing to speak too stiffly unless that it be feasible to carry out thy words.

T. W. Rolleston, MYTHS AND LEGENDS OF THE CELTIC RACE

That conversation, where the spirit of raillery is
    suppressed,
    will ever appear tedious and insipid.

Richard Brinsley Sheridan, THE SCHOOL FOR SCANDAL

We find ourselves in the atmosphere of a tempest – every word of reason is suppressed or distorted until it is made to appear the voice of passion.

Eamon de Valera, IRISH INDEPENDENT, *10 March 1923*

I know everybody worth knowing in Europe. I have been everywhere, eaten everything, and seen everything. There's not a railway guard doesn't give a recognition to me; not a waiter, from the Trois Frères to the Wilde Mann, doesn't trail his napkin to earth as he sees me. Ministers speak up when I stroll into the Chamber, and prima donnas soar above the orchestra as I enter the pit.

Charles Lever writing as 'Cornelius O'Dowd', ESSAYS

I cannot thank you: silence is the gratitude of true affection: who seeks to follow it by sound will miss the track.

Richard Brinsley Sheridan, PIZARRO

Silence gives meaning
   to the language of the eyes;
   and silence of the lips cannot keep
   the secret that a glance betrays.

Niall More MacMurray, 'Farewell to Last Night' (trans. Myles Dillon)

Guard for me my tongue, that I slander no man, that I revile no one, that I vaunt not swearingly.

Máel Ísu Úa Brolchán, 'Lord, Guard me' (trans. Gerard Murphy)

But surely unto Thee mine eyes did show
   Why I am silent, and my lute unstrung;
   Else it were better we should part, and go,
   Thou to some lips of sweeter melody,
   And I to nurse the barren memory
   Of unkissed kisses, and songs never sung.

Oscar Wilde, 'Silentium Amoris'

A good speaker in Ireland is not a man who talks keen sense well, but one with 'the divil's flow of words'.

D. P. Moran, 'The Battle of Two Civilizations'

The Infinite always is silent:
   It is only the Finite speaks.

John Boyle O'Reilly, 'The Infinite'

the mouth that speaks not is sweet to hear.

An Irish proverb

Soul has its scruples. Things not to be said
    Things for keeping, that can keep the small-hours gaze
    Open and steady. Things for the aye of God
    And for poetry. Which is, as Milosz says,
    'A dividend from ourselves,' a tribute paid
    By what we have been true to. A thing allowed.

Seamus Heaney, 'On His Work in the English Tongue', in memory of
Ted Hughes

Eloquence smooth and cutting, is like a Razor whetted with Oil.

Jonathan Swift, 'Thoughts on Various Subjects'

My hand is weary with writing; my sharp great point is
    not thick; my slender-beaked pen juts forth a beetle-
    hued draught of bright blue ink.

A steady stream of wisdom springs from my well-
    coloured neat fair hand; on the page it pours its
    draught of ink of the green-skinned holly.

I send my little dripping pen unceasingly over an
    assemblage of books of great beauty, to enrich the
    possessions of men of art – whence my hand is
    weary with writing.

Attributed to St Columcille, 'My Hand Is Weary with Writing' (trans.
Gerard Murphy)

Only the great masters of style ever succeed in being obscure.

Oscar Wilde, 'Phrases and Philosophies for the use of the Young'

wit and humour

for surely if humour be not an actual virtue, it is one of the chief among the graces and the charms of life, and its demise demands a tear.

George Townshend, THE GENIUS OF IRELAND

Of the things which nourish the imagination humour is one of the most needful, and it is dangerous to limit or destroy it.

J. M. Synge, preface to The Tinker's Wedding

In Ireland the inevitable never happens but the impossible always does.

John P. Mahaffy as quoted by Des MacHale

You've got to do your own growing no matter how tall your grandfather was.

Quoted by Sean McCann

never before had I believed or suspected that I had a soul but just then I knew I had. I knew also that my soul was friendly, was my senior in years and was solely concerned for my own welfare. For convenience I called him Joe. I felt a little reassured to know that I was not altogether alone. Joe was helping me.

Flann O'Brien, THE THIRD POLICEMAN

You haven't an arm and you haven't a leg,
  You're an eyeless, noseless, chickenless egg;
  You'll have to be put with a bowl to beg:
  Och, Johnny, I hardly knew ye!

'Johnny, I Hardly Knew Ye!' an Irish ballad

'Whisht, whisht, Paddy,' says the captain, 'don't be talkin' bad of any one,' says he; 'you don't know how soon you may want a good word put in for yourself, if you should be called to quarters in th' other world all of a suddint,' says he.

Samuel Lover, THE GRIDIRON

You're too big for one bite, and too small for two.

Jeremiah Curtin, THE SHEE AN GANNON AND THE GRUAGACH GAIRE

What goes out at the ebb comes in on the flood.

Lady Gregory, THE WHITE COCKADE

If it's a poor thing to be lonesome, it's worse maybe go mixing with the fools of earth.

J. M. Synge, THE PLAYBOY OF THE WESTERN WORLD

- Three slender things that best support the world: the slender stream of milk from the cow's dug into the pail; the slender blade of green corn upon the ground; the slender thread over the hand of a skilled woman.

- Three rude ones of the world: a youngster mocking an old man; a robust person mocking an invalid; a wise man mocking a fool.

- Three fair things that hide ugliness: good manners in the ill-favoured; skill in a serf; wisdom in the misshapen.

- Three glories of a gathering: a beautiful wife, a good horse, a swift hound.

- Three signs of a fop: the track of his comb in his hair; the track of his teeth in his food; the track of his stick behind him.

- Three idiots of a bad guest-house: an old hag with a chronic cough; a brainless tartar of a girl; a hobgoblin of a gilly.

- Three things that constitute a physician: a complete cure; leaving no blemish behind; a painless examination.

- Three nurses of theft: a wood, a cloak, night.

- Three false sisters: 'Perhaps', 'Maybe', 'I dare say'.

- Three timid brothers: 'Hush!' 'Stop!' 'Listen!'

- Three sounds of increase: the lowing of a cow in milk; the din of a smithy; the swish of a plough.

- Three steadinesses of good womanhood: keeping a steady tongue, a steady chastity, a steady housewifery.

- Three candles that illume every darkness: truth, nature, knowledge.

- Three keys that unlock thoughts: drunkenness, trustfulness, love.

- Three youthful sisters: desire, beauty, generosity.

- Three aged sisters: groaning, chastity, ugliness.

- Three services, the worst that a man can serve: serving a bad woman, a bad lord, and bad land.

Anonymous, 'Triads of Ireland' (trans. Kuno Meyer)

> *Joseph S.:* But, my dear Lady Teazle, 'tis your own fault if you suffer it. When a husband entertains a groundless suspicion of his wife, and withdraws his confidence from her, the original compact is broke, and she owes it to the honour of her sex to endeavour to outwit him.
>
> *Lady T.:* Indeed! – so that if he suspects me without cause, it follows, that the best way of curing his jealousy is to give him reason for't.

Richard Brinsley Sheridan, THE SCHOOL FOR SCANDAL

the first beginnings of wisdom ... is to ask questions but never to answer any. *You* get wisdom from asking and *I* from not answering.

Flann O'Brien, THE THIRD POLICEMAN

It's many times there's more sense in madmen than the wise.

J. M. Synge, DEIRDRE OF THE SORROWS

a man in the professions can never lose. A lawyer is paid – win or lose. A doctor is paid – kill or cure. A priest is paid – heaven or hell.

An Irish farmer quoted by Sean McCann

nothing makes one so vain as being told that one is a sinner. Conscience makes egotists of us all.

Oscar Wilde, The Picture of Dorian Gray

In wealth, many friends. In poverty not even relatives.

Quoted by Sean McCann

Wit loses its respect with me, when I see it in company with malice.

Richard Brinsley Sheridan, The School for Scandal

Pickering: Have you no morals, man?

Doolittle: Can't afford them, Governor. Neither could you if you was as poor as me.

George Bernard Shaw, Pygmalion

We are little airy creatures,
　　All of different voice and features;
　　One of us in glass is set,
　　One of us you'll find in jet.
　　T'other you may see in tin,
　　And the fourth a box within.
　　If the fifth you should pursue,
　　It can never fly from you.

Jonathan Swift, '[The Vowels:] A Riddle'

never take for a wife a woman who has no faults.

Quoted by Sean McCann

It was explained what was upside-down and amiss and back-to-front with Corkadoragha as a centre of learning. It appeared that:

1. The tempest of the countryside was too tempestuous.
2. The putridity of the countryside was too putrid.
3. The poverty of the countryside was too poor.
4. The Gaelicism of the countryside was too Gaelic.
5. The tradition of the countryside was too traditional.

Flann O'Brien, THE POOR MOUTH

Edwin and Angela are twins,
    And often kick each other's shins,
    But haven't hurt each other yet
    Their boots are made of flannel-ette!
    They try to pull each other's hair,
    But soon desist in sheer despair,
    For hair is very hard to pull
    When hands are cased in Berlin wool.

Percy French, 'Bad Ballads for Badish Babies: No. 2 The Infantile Tyrannical'

There's no bad publicity except an obituary.

Brendan Behan as quoted by Sean McCann

I don't know who it is
    that Étan is going to sleep with.
    But I know the lovely Étan
    will not be sleeping alone.

Anonymous, 'The Lovely Étan' (trans. Thomas Kinsella)

Louis XIV asked Count Mahoney if he understood Italian: Yes, please, Your Majesty, if it's spoken in Irish.

Quoted by Sean McCann

The boy is so full of sport that I believe he would sing at his own funeral.

Dion Boucicault, THE SHAUGHRAUN

Jocasta Jinks had one reply
　　To ev'rything; and that was "Why?"
　　Her parents were extremely poor
　　In ev'rything, except in children to be sure.

They had a dozen girls and boys
　　Who wanted food and clothes and toys
　　One day her father whisper'd "Come and see
　　What Heaven has sent to you and me."
　　Jocasta gazed with look intent
　　Upon the babe that Heav'n had sent
　　And when Jocasta murmur'd – "Why?"
　　Her Pa and Ma made no reply.

Percy French, 'Bad Ballads for Badish Babies: No. 4 The Absolutely Unanswerable'

In the foyer of the Cork House after the première of one of his plays, a lady with an umbrella stopped J B Keane and berated him publicly. 'Stand there', she shouted, prodding him with the umbrella, 'till I give you a piece of my mind.'

'My dear woman, your mind is so small that if you give me a bit of it you wouldn't have any left for yourself.'

Quoted by Sean McCann

Long life to you, sir, and may you never see your wife a widow.

A beggar's blessing quoted by Sean McCann

The life of a bill collector isn't all that bad. Almost everyone asks him to call again.

Irish Saying, IRISH DIGEST, *May 1967*

When I was meditating ... I took all my sins out and put them on the table, so to speak. I need not tell you it was a big table.

Flann O'Brien, THE THIRD POLICEMAN

It's little you'll think if my love's a poacher's or an earl's itself when you'll feel my two hands stretched around you, and I squeezing kisses on your puckered lips till I'd feel a kind of pity for the Lord God is all ages sitting lonesome in his golden chair.

J. M. Synge, THE PLAYBOY OF THE WESTERN WORLD

ethics

virtue and ethics

Good manners chiefly consist in action, not in words. Modesty and humility the chief ingredients.

Jonathan Swift, 'Hints on Good Manners'

"Virtue," said he, "is the performance of pleasant actions."

James Stephens, THE CROCK OF GOLD

Contented toil, and hospitable care,
And kind connubial tenderness, are there;
And piety with wishes placed above,
And steady loyalty, and faithful love.

Oliver Goldsmith, 'The Deserted Village'

We can only try because perseverance is its own reward and necessity is the unmarried mother of invention.

Flann O'Brien, THE THIRD POLICEMAN

nothing less than this could render it pardonable to have recourse to those old-fashioned trite maxims concerning religion, industry, frugality, and public spirit which are now forgotten, but, if revived and put in practice, may not only prevent our final ruin, but also render us a more happy and flourishing people than ever.

George Berkeley, 'An Essay Towards Preventing the Ruin of Great Britain'

The old days are over: how pleasant they were while
    they lasted!
    The sands were pure gold that ran out ere we knew
    they were wasted.
    And still I'm forgetting, ochone, that no longer
    you're near me,
    And turn to you still with my tale, and there's no one
    to hear me.

Katherine Tynan, 'Everything That I Made'

a good action is its own reward.

Dion Boucicault, THE SHAUGHRAUN

The good are real as the sun,
    Are best perceived through clouds
    Of casual corruption
    That cannot kill the luminous sufficiency
    That shines on city, sea and wilderness,
    Fastidiously revealing
    One man to another,
    Who yet will not accept
    Responsibilities of light.

Brendan Kennelly, 'The Good'

no good comes of money that you don't work for.

George Moore, ESTHER WATERS

a virtue must be made of necessity.

An Irish proverb

"AND WHAT would you call wisdom?"

"I couldn't rightly say now," he replied, "but I think it was not to mind about the world, and not to care whether you were hungry or not, and not to live in the world at all but only in your own head, for the world is a tyrannous place. You have to raise yourself above things instead of letting things raise themselves above you. We must not be slaves to each other, and we must not be slaves to our necessities either. That is the problem of existence. There is no dignity in life at all if hunger can shout 'stop' at every turn of the road and the day's journey is measured by the distance between one sleep and the next sleep."

James Stephens, THE CROCK OF GOLD

Virtue has in herself the most engaging charms.

George Berkeley, 'The Sanctions of Religion'

In the meantime we are born only to be men. We shall do enough if we form ourselves to be good ones. It is therefore our business carefully to cultivate in our minds, to rear to the most perfect vigour and maturity, every sort of generous and honest feeling that belongs to our nature.

Edmund Burke, 'Thoughts on the Cause of the Present Discontents, 1770'

patience is a poultice for all wounds.

An Irish proverb

To break a man's spirit is devil's work.

George Bernard Shaw, CANDIDA

Instead of dirt and poison we have rather chosen to fill our hives with honey and wax; thus furnishing mankind with the two noblest of things, which are sweetness and light.

Jonathan Swift, THE BATTLE OF THE BOOKS

I summon to-day all these powers between me and
      those evils,
   Against every cruel merciless power that may oppose
      my body and soul,
   Against incantations of false prophets,
   Against black laws of pagandom,
   Against false laws of heretics,
   Against craft of idolatry,
   Against spells of women and smiths and wizards,
   Against every knowledge that corrupts man's body
      and soul.

Attributed to St Patrick, 'The Deer's Cry' (trans. Kuno Meyer)

Always forgive your enemies; nothing annoys them so much.

Oscar Wilde as quoted by Sean McCann

Be no frequenter of the drinking-house, nor given to carping at the old; meddle not with a man of mean estate.

T. W. Rolleston, MYTHS AND LEGENDS OF THE CELTIC RACE

The lucky man waits for prosperity.

An Irish proverb

Shutting our eyes to facts will not change the facts.

George Moore, SALVE

Whenever a stranger
Come 'mid thy possessions,
   Shield him from danger,
And guard him from wrong;
Let courtesy sit in thy heart and thy brow,
Let him be gladdened, but thou
Hast duties, so wield them – ...

Be sparing of words,
Be calm and not loud in thy speech;
   Loving to think – ...

My son!
Be thou kindly disposed towards all; –
Thinking evil of none,
Till their deeds show their sorrowful fall;
Do evil to none,
From those who offend thee demand
Not things over bitter to bear.
Be gentle, be merciful, and
   Open of hand.
If thou hast wronged any, by chance,
Be not shamed, but declare
Thine error, and yield him his share. ...

Bear with them, bear for them, endure
   Much that their circle increase
In purity, honour, and peace.
   With thy foes
Be strong, word-keeping, and sure.
Be courteous, nor taunt with their woes
Those who have suffered defeat.

Anonymous, 'The King's Lay' (trans. George Sigerson)

Whoever is patient … is satisfied.

Flann O'Brien, THE POOR MOUTH

Decency is not clothing but Mind. Morality is behaviour. Virtue is thought.

James Stephens, THE CROCK OF GOLD

nothing can be more short-sighted than cunning.

Maria Edgeworth, THE WHITE PIGEON

hate, I suggest, inspires nothing but destruction.

D. P. Moran, 'The Battle of Two Civilizations'

> Look not with pride at thy polished shoe,
>   Be not proud, too, of thy cloak so nice,
>   In humility walk the road afoot,
>   And always salute the poor man twice.

Anonymous, 'Look Not' (trans. Douglas Hyde)

I say nothing – I take away from no man's merit – am hurt at no man's good fortune – I say nothing – But this I will say – through all my knowledge of life, I have observed – that there is not a passion so strongly rooted in the human heart as envy!

Richard Brinsley Sheridan, THE CRITIC

You can't let a boy grow up naturally. He must be brought up in some theory of what is right and what is wrong.

George Moore, SALVE

It is neither wise nor just, to judge of any set of people by an individual, whether that individual be good or bad.

Maria Edgeworth, Mademoiselle Panache

But my code is a simple one, and, I think, a good one. Honor between man and man; fidelity between man and woman; and no cant about this religion or that religion, but an honest belief that things are making for good on the whole.

George Bernard Shaw, Mrs. Warren's Profession

You are the most patient man in the world today. Therefore, you will have a long life. Fate will never kill you for your Patience has defeated it.

From an Irish legend (trans. Sean O'Sullivan)

Man's doom is doubtful; but one thing is clear:
    That Good beats Evil down in spite of skaith;
And when I come across a man like you
    Serene amid the discord and sincere,
    Belief in human nature cheers anew
By re-confirming, when it flags, my faith.

Oliver St John Gogarty, 'To Major Eugene F. Kinkead'

What is right should not only be made known, but made prevalent; that what is evil should not only be detected, but defeated.

Edmund Burke, 'Thoughts on the Cause of the Present Discontents, 1770'

For what cannot be cured patience is the best remedy.

An Irish proverb

hospitality and generosity

G od shares with the person who is generous.

An Irish proverb

No man has ever passed my gate
 Or asked help at my open door
 But he has had it, early, late,
 Friend he, or foe, or rich or poor.
 Yes, if the food was at its last,
 In time of storm or siege or war
 The King himself would sooner fast
 Than let a dog go famine sore.
 Never till now has it been said
 That Guaire has a narrow heart –
 That of his meat and of his bread
 He would not share one smallest part.

Lady Gregory, COLMAN AND GUAIRE

You are an ill-mannered people, not to ask a stranger is he hungry or dry!

Jeremiah Curtin, GILLA NA GRAKIN AND FIN MacCUMHAIL

You must be fit to give before you can be fit to receive.

James Stephens, THE CROCK OF GOLD

A princely upright hundred-herd brugaid was born one time in the lovely province of Connaught, namely, Conall Derg O'Corra the fair-haired. And thus was this brugaid (circumstanced):– he was a fortunate, rich, prosperous man; and his house was never found without three shouts in it – the shout of the brewers brewing ale, and the shout of the servants over the caldrons distributing (meat) to the hosts, and the shout of the youths over the chessboards winning games from one another.

The same house was never without three measures:– a measure of malt for making yeast, a measure of wheat for providing bread for the guests, and a measure of salt for savouring each kind of food.

P. W. Joyce, OLD CELTIC ROMANCES

The overpaying instinct is a generous one: better than the underpaying instinct, and not so common.

George Bernard Shaw, CANDIDA

We think that we are generous because we credit our neighbour with the possession of those virtues that are likely to be a benefit to us.

Oscar Wilde, THE PICTURE OF DORIAN GRAY

Be more apt to give than to deny, and follow after gentleness.

T. W. Rolleston, Myths and Legends of the Celtic Race

His tables are still spread with food; he bade me
    Welcome all strangers coming to his court.
His name goes far beyond the bounds of Aidne,
    Guaire, whose bounty gilds the name of Gort.

Lady Gregory, Colman and Guaire

O King of stars!
    Whether my house be dark or bright,
    Never shall it be closed against any one,
    Lest Christ close His house against me.

If there be a guest in your house
    And you conceal aught from him,
    'Tis not the guest that will be without it,
    But Jesus, Mary's Son.

Anonymous, 'Hospitality' (trans. Kuno Meyer)

Finn taught to all his followers, and the best of them became like himself in valour and gentleness and generosity. Each of them loved the repute of his comrades more than his own, and each would say that for all noble qualities there was no man in the breadth of the world worthy to be thought of beside Finn.

It was said of him that 'he gave away gold as if it were the leaves of the woodland, and silver as if it were the foam of the sea'; and that whatever he had bestowed upon any man, if he fell out with him afterwards, he was never known to bring it against him.

T. W. Rolleston, Myths and Legends of the Celtic Race

The wedding was over a week and a day
  Before the last guest could be driven away;
  For everyone's going he tried to retard:
  "What ails ye?" said Croker of Ballinagarde.

Oliver St John Gogarty, 'Croker of Ballinagarde'

G ive a welcome to the man that is coming towards you.

Lady Gregory, GODS AND FIGHTING MEN

There shall be peace and plenty – the kindly open door;
  Blessings on all who come and go – the prosperous
  or the poor.

Ethna Carbery, 'Mo Chraoibhin Cno'

'W elcome, friend Fergus,' Cúchulainn said. 'If the salmon were swimming in the rivers or river-mouths I'd give you one and share another. If a flock of wild birds were to alight on the plain I'd give you one and share another; with a handful of cress or sea-herb and a handful of marshwort; and a drink out of the sand; and myself in your place in the ford of battle, watching while you slept.'

TÁIN BÓ CUAILNGE *(trans. Thomas Kinsella)*

Enough, I do not need so much beseeching,
  All men in want are welcome in my sight;
  But tell me what his race, that I outreaching
  My hand to him, may honour him aright.

Lady Gregory, COLMAN AND GUAIRE

h elping others, that is the only happiness.

George Moore, ESTHER WATERS

Ask not a favour
Again, if refused thee at first;
For the mind becomes mean,
If the heart be a craver.

Anonymous, 'The King's Lay' (trans. George Sigerson)

There stood near the fire a small round table, covered with a snow-white cloth, upon which shone in unrivalled brightness a very handsome tea equipage – the hissing kettle on one hob was *vis-à-vis*'d by a gridiron with three newly taken trout frying under the reverential care of Father Malachi himself – a heap of eggs, ranged like shot in an ordnance yard, stood in the middle of the table, while a formidable pile of buttered toast browned before the grate – the morning papers were airing upon the hearth – everything bespoke that attention to comfort and enjoyment one likes to discover in the house where chance may have domesticated him for a day or two.

Charles Lever, THE CONFESSIONS OF HARRY LORREQUER

learning, knowledge and their virtues

Knowledge comes through practice.

An Irish proverb

a country without teaching is not a real country, but a piece of earth on which a lot of people are set, without knowledge of the good beyond the bad, or of truth beyond falsehood.

Douglas Hyde, 'What Ireland is Asking for' (trans. Lady Gregory)

> Take a copious draught each day
> from wisdom's noble spring.
>   It won't taste sour in your mouth.
>   Knowledge is a hold on bliss.

Anonymous, 'Every Morning, My Young Lad'
(trans. Thomas Kinsella)

Learning comes through work.

An Irish proverb

I t is seldom your knowledge fails you.

Lady Gregory, Gods and Fighting Men

t he greatest of all virtues is curiosity, and the end of all desire is wisdom.

James Stephens, The Crock of Gold

A man without guidance is weak,
Blind are all the ignorant.

Attributed to St Columcille, 'Columcille's Greeting to Ireland' (trans. Kuno Meyer)

t o cease to study life is to turn away from the chief source of knowledge available.

William Larminie, 'Legends as Material for Literature'

The man whose learning's best
is often lacking in precision,
but his understanding's deeper
because his heart keeps singing,
while I for facts keep searching
and I examine them minutely,
because th' original fault ancestral
of the banished sons of Adam
is to seek out the tree of knowledge
and give the tree of life the slip,
since her spouse in hand so sinful
took from Mother Eve the apple
and ate with no examination
the wrong tree's fruit.

Gearóid Ó Clérigh, 'Fruit of Two Trees' (trans. by the author)

praise the young and they will blossom.

An Irish proverb

a child may learn as much from conversation as from books, not so many historic facts, but as much instruction.

Maria Edgeworth, THE GOOD AUNT

knowledge opens up new avenues of satisfaction, and effort keeps one's enjoyment fresh.

George Townshend, THE GENIUS OF IRELAND

there is no country on the earth in which either education, or the desire to procure it, is so much reverenced as in Ireland. Next to the claims of the priest and schoolmaster come those of the poor scholar for the respect of the people. It matters not how poor or how miserable he may be; so long as they see him struggling with poverty in the prosecution of a purpose so laudable, they will treat him with attention and kindness. Here there is no danger of his being sent to the workhouse, committed as a vagrant – or passed from parish to parish until he reaches his own settlement. Here the humble lad is not met by the sneer of purse-proud insolence, or his simple tale answered only by the frown of heartless contempt. No – no – no. The best bit and sup are placed before him; and whilst his poor, but warm-hearted entertainer can afford only potatoes and salt to his own half-starved family, he will make a struggle to procure something better for the poor scholar; "*Bekase he's far from his own, the crathur! An' sure the intintion in him is good, any how; the Lord prosper him, an' every one that has the heart set upon the larnin'!*"

William Carleton, 'The Poor Scholar'

We phone, write letters, prowl through books,
    dream of losing, winning
    love and fortune. And always, always,
    the adventure is beginning.

Brendan Kennelly, 'The Adventure of Learning'

I have lived in important places, times
    When great events were decided: who owned
    That half a rood of rock, a no-man's land
    Surrounded by our pitchfork-armed claims.
    I heard the Duffys shouting 'Damn your soul'
    And old McCabe stripped to the waist, seen
    Step the plot defying blue cast-steel –
    'Here is the march along these iron stones'
    That was the year of the Munich bother. Which
    Was most important? I inclined
    To lose my faith in Ballyrush and Gortin
    Till Homer's ghost came whispering to my mind
    He said: I made the Iliad from such
    A local row. Gods make their own importance.

Patrick Kavanagh, 'Epic'

Education is an admirable thing. But it is well to remember from time to time that nothing that is worth knowing can be taught.

Oscar Wilde, 'A Few Maxims for the Instruction of the Over-Educated'

Prudence, like experience, must be paid for.

Richard Brinsley Sheridan, THE SCHOOL FOR SCANDAL

The student's life is pleasant
    And pleasant is his labour,
  Search all Ireland over,
    You'll find no better neighbour.

Nor lords nor petty princes
    Dispute the student's pleasure,
  Nor chapter stints his purse
    Nor stewardship his leisure.

Anonymous, 'The Student' (trans. Frank O'Connor)

as the old cock crows the young cock learns.

An Irish saying

Oh! knowledge is a wondrous power, and stronger than
    the wind;
And thrones shall fall, and despots bow, before the
    might of mind;
The poet and the orator the heart of man can sway,
And would to the kind heavens that Wolfe Tone were
    here to-day
Yet trust me, friends, dear Ireland's strength – her
    truest strength is still
The rough and ready roving boys, like Rory of the
    Hill!

Charles Kickham, 'Rory of the Hills'

I am sure for a child to spend all day in school with a stupid, ill-trained man under an ill-planned system, is less good for that child than that the child should be running through the fields and learning nothing.

W. B. Yeats, 'Condition of Schools', 24 March 1926

a man might be a great scholar, without being a man of sense.

Maria Edgeworth, THE GOOD AUNT

p hilosophy being nothing else but the study of wisdom and truth, it may with reason be expected, that those who have spent most time and pains in it should enjoy a greater calm and serenity of mind, a greater clearness and evidence of knowledge, and be less disturbed with doubts and difficulties than other men. Yet so it is we see the illiterate bulk of mankind that walk the high-road of plain, common sense, and are governed by the dictates of Nature, for the most part easy and undisturbed. To them nothing that's familiar appears unaccountable or difficult to comprehend.

George Berkeley, Introduction to 'A Treatise concerning the Principles of Human Knowledge'

e xperience is the name which everyone gives to his mistakes.

Oscar Wilde as quoted by Sean McCann

loyalty, friendship and honouring one's obligation

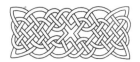

I don't pretend that I had not moments of trial and temptation, but I do claim that never in thought, word, or deed, have I been false to the trust which Irishmen have confided in me.

Charles Stewart Parnell at a meeting in the Rotunda,
18 December 1890

So long as thou shalt live, thy lord forsake not; neither for gold nor for other reward in the world abandon one whom thou art pledged to protect.

T. W. Rolleston, Myths and Legends of the Celtic Race

The love of praise and esteem may do something: but to make a true patriot there must be an inward sense of duty and conscience.

George Berkeley, 'Maxims concerning Patriotism'

The thread of our life would be dark, Heaven knows!
　　If it were not with friendship and love
　　　intertwined.

Thomas Moore, 'Oh Think not My Spirits are Always as Light'

Scully! thou false one,
　　You basely betray'd him;
　　In his strong hour of need
　　　When thy right hand should aid him;
　　He fed thee; – he clad thee; –
　　　You had all could delight thee;
　　You left him; – you sold him; –
　　　May Heaven requite thee!

Jeremiah Joseph Callanan, 'Dirge of O'Sullivan Bear'

"**W**ell," said Gilla, "I never knew that you wanted to put me to death till this minute; I know it now. But still so long as I'm in your service I can't refuse to do your work."

Jeremiah Curtin, Gilla na Grakin and Fin MacCumhail

anyone without a soul-friend is like a body without a head.

A folk saying (trans. Thomas Cahill)

Oh! sons and daughters of the coming age,
　　Give worthy meed of gratitude and praise
　　To those true souls who, in less happy days,
　　Have lived for others – most of all for you –
　　Have stored the wealth which is your heritage,
　　And planned the work it will be yours to do.

John Kells Ingram, 'The Social Future'

There is not strength without unity.

An Irish proverb

I never will join in ridiculing a friend.

Richard Brinsley Sheridan, THE SCHOOL FOR SCANDAL

Burdens rest heaviest on the shoulders of people who are best able to bear them and rest lightest on the shoulders of those least able to bear them. ... Every member of the community has to bear his part of the burden.

Eamon de Valera, Dáil Éireann debate, 29 April 1932

Contempt on the minion who calls you disloyal!
        Though fierce to your foe, to your friends you are
        true;
And the tribute most high to a head that is royal,
        Is love from a heart that loves liberty too.

Thomas Moore, 'The Prince's Day'

You can't come over to my side, so I'll come over to your side.

Frank O'Connor, 'Guests of the Nation'

Woe to him who fails in his obligations.

An Irish proverb

I never meddle with any man's secrets, that he does not choose to trust me with.

Maria Edgeworth, FORGIVE AND FORGET

Break not your vows.

An Irish proverb

Thank God for one dear friend,
With face still radiant with the light of truth,
Whose love comes laden with the scent of youth,
Through twenty years of death.

John Boyle O'Reilly, 'Forever'

We are all brothers in this, that no one of us can suffer for any length of time without that suffering reflecting on the rest of us. It is our duty to stand together.

Eamon de Valera, speaking at College Green, Dublin to explain the economic war

It would be well for all the world, if they could be convinced … that to live in friendship is better than to quarrel.

Maria Edgeworth, FORGIVE AND FORGET

daily life

men and women

When lovely woman stoops to folly,
    And finds too late that men betray,
    What charm can soothe her melancholy,
    What art can wash her guilt away?

The only art her guilt to cover,
    To hide her shame from every eye,
    To give repentance to her lover,
    And wring his bosom, is – to die

Oliver Goldsmith, 'Stanzas on Woman'

marriage is the earliest fruit of civilisation and it will be the latest. I think a man and a woman should choose each other for life, for the simple reason that a long life with all its accidents is barely long enough for a man and woman to understand each other; and in this case, to understand is to love. The man who understands one woman is qualified to understand pretty well anything.

John Butler Yeats as quoted by Sean McCann

People seem to me to have quite forgotten *what a wife is*. A man may admire one woman and be in love with another, and all sorts of wanton fancies in his restless heart may play continually about a third. There is one woman whom *he accepts* and she is his wife – all her limitations, her want of intellect, even her want of heart. All her infirmities and all her waywardness he accepts and would not have them altered. If there be such a woman she is his wife. The feeling grows slowly. It is not affection as it is not passion. It is just *husband's feeling*, and she has doubtless a corresponding *wife's feeling*.

John Butler Yeats, letter to W. B. Yeats, 15 January 1916

> Women are stronger than men – they do not die of
>   wisdom.
>   They are better than men because they do not seek
>   wisdom.
>   They are wiser than men because they know less and
>   understand more.

James Stephens, THE CROCK OF GOLD

Educating her for the Harem, but calling on her for the practices of the Portico, man expects from his odalisque the firmness of the stoic, and demands from his servant the exercise of those virtues which, placing the *élite* of his own sex at the head of its muster-roll, give immortality to the master. He tells her 'that obscurity is *her* true glory, insignificance her distinction, ignorance her lot, and passive obedience the perfection of her nature;' yet he expects from her … that conquest over the passions by the strength of reason, that triumph of moral energy over the senses and their appetites, and that endurance of personal privations and self-denials, which with him … are qualities of rare exception, the practices of most painful acquirement.

Lady Morgan, WOMAN AND HER MASTER

Disguise our bondage as we will,
'Tis woman, woman, rules us still.

Thomas Moore, 'Sovereign Woman'

two-thirds of thy gentleness be shown to women and to those that creep on the floor (little children) and to poets, and be not violent to the common people.

T. W. Rolleston, Myths and Legends of the Celtic Race

Lady T.: Women of fashion … are accountable to nobody after they are married.

Sir Peter T.: Very well, ma'am, very well; – so a husband is to have no influence, no authority?

Lady T.: Authority! No, to be sure: – if you wanted authority over me, you should have adopted me, and not married me.

Richard Brinsley Sheridan, The School for Scandal

Woe to him who does not follow the advice of a good wife!

P. W. Joyce, Old Celtic Romances

What woman is there that a man can trust
But at the moment when he kisses her
At the first midnight?

W. B. Yeats, Deirdre

a gentleman has no right to hurt a woman under any circumstances.

George Bernard Shaw, Arms and the Man

Boxty on the griddle, Boxty in the pan,
    If you don't eat Boxty you'll never get a man.

An Irish saying

most men have notions before they marry: but they are soon brought to their senses, if their wives are clever.

Edward Martyn, THE HEATHER FIELD

Oh! light and false is a young man's kiss,
    And a foolish girl gives her soul for this.
    Oh! light and short is the young man's blame,
    And a helpless girl has the grief and shame.

William Allingham, 'The Girls' Lamentation'

men are not fathers by instinct but by chance, but women are mothers beyond thought, beyond instinct which is the father of thought.

James Stephens, THE CROCK OF GOLD

We'll be all right, it's the women who will suffer. The worst they can do to us is kill us, but the women will have to remain behind to rear the children.

Eamon de Valera, as quoted by J. O'Connor in 'The rising by the river', in IRISH PRESS, *14 April 1950*

I find that the moment I let a woman make friends with me, she becomes jealous, exacting, suspicious, and a damned nuisance. I find that the moment I let myself make friends with a woman, I become selfish and tyrannical.

George Bernard Shaw, PYGMALION

I am the pillars of the house;
    The keystone of the arch am I.
Take me away, and roof and wall
    Would fall to ruin utterly.

I am the fire upon the hearth,
    I am the light of the good sun,
I am the heat that warms the earth,
    Which else were colder than a stone.

At me the children warm their hands;
    I am their light of love alive.
Without me cold the hearthstone stands,
    Nor could the precious children thrive.

I am the twist that holds together
    The children in its sacred ring,
Their knot of love, from whose close tether
    No lost child goes a-wandering.

I am the house from floor to roof,
    I deck the walls, the board I spread;
I spin the curtains, warp and woof,
    And shake the down to be their bed.

I am their wall against all danger,
    Their door against the wind and snow,
Thou Whom a woman laid in manger,
    Take me not till the children grow!

Katherine Tynan, 'Any Woman'

Well! woman is a wonderful and mysterious thing!

Dion Boucicault, OLD HEADS AND YOUNG HEARTS

a misanthrope I can understand – a womanthrope, never.

Oscar Wilde as quoted by Sean McCann

the six gifts of womanhood – the gift of beauty, the gift of voice, the gift of sweet speech, the gift of needlework, the gift of wisdom, and the gift of chastity.

T. W. Rolleston, Myths and Legends of the Celtic Race

Get married to a good woman; and then you'll understand. That's a foretaste of what will be best in the Kingdom of Heaven we are trying to establish on earth.

George Bernard Shaw, Candida

If you marry the right woman there is nothing like it and if you marry the wrong woman there is nothing like it.

Quoted by Sean McCann

men, not women, are riddles.

Richard Brinsley Sheridan, A Trip to Scarborough

love and romance

Man is in love and loves what vanishes,
What more is there to say?

W. B. Yeats, 'Nineteen Hundred and Nineteen'

h atred is the destroyer of peace for men; love, of their integrity.

St Columbanus, addressed to Attala (trans. Eleanor Shipley Duckett)

Surely Love is a wonderful thing. It is more precious than emeralds, and dearer than fine opals. Pearls and pomegranates cannot buy it, nor is it set forth in the market-place. It may not be purchased of the merchants, nor can it be weighed out in the balance for gold.

Oscar Wilde, THE NIGHTINGALE AND THE ROSE

O, My Dark Rosaleen,
    Do not sigh, do not weep!
The priests are on the ocean green,
    They march along the Deep.
There's wine from the royal Pope,
    Upon the ocean green;
And Spanish ale shall give you hope,
    My Dark Rosaleen!
    My own Rosaleen!
Shall glad your heart, shall give you hope,
Shall give you health, and help, and hope,
    My Dark Rosaleen!

Over hills, and through dales,
    Have I roamed for your sake;
All yesterday I sailed with sails
    On river and on lake.
The Erne, at its highest flood,
    I dashed across unseen,
For there was lightning in my blood,
    My Dark Rosaleen!
    My own Rosaleen!
Oh! there was lightning in my blood,
Red lightning lightened through my blood,
    My Dark Rosaleen!

All day long, in unrest,
    To and fro, do I move.
The very soul within my breast
    Is wasted for you, love!
The heart in my bosom faints
    To think of you, my Queen,
My life of life, my saint of saints,
    My Dark Rosaleen!
    My own Rosaleen!
To hear your sweet and sad complaints,

My life, my love, my saint of saints,
   My Dark Rosaleen!

James Clarence Mangan, 'Dark Rosaleen' (trans by the author)

I love my love in the morning,
   For she like morn is fair –
Her blushing cheek, its crimson streak,
   It clouds her golden hair.
Her glance, its beam, so soft and kind;
   Her tears, its dewy showers;
And her voice, the tender whispering wind
   That stirs the early bowers.

Gerald Griffin, 'I Love My Love in the Morning'

There is one
   On whom I should gladly gaze,
   For whom I would give the bright world,
   All of it, all of it, though it be an unequal bargain.

Anonymous, 'The Glories of Colum Cille' (trans. Gerard Murphy)

Death is friendlier than love.

From bardic poetry (trans. Eleanor Knott)

Two women loved him, shapes of Heaven,
   Radiant as aught beneath the sky.
      One gentle as the summer moon
      One ardent as the golden noon;
   And to the first his heart was given,
      And to the last his vanity.

Thomas Caulfield Irwin, 'Swift'

It was not the grace of her queenly air,
    Nor her cheek of the roses' glow,
    Nor her soft black eyes,
    Nor her flowing hair,
    Nor was it her lily-white brow.
'Twas the soul of truth
And of melting ruth,
And the smile of summer's dawn,
That stole my heart away,
One mild summer day
In the valley near Slievenamon.

'Slievenamon', an Irish song

The sighing wind dies on the tree.
    I cannot sigh: sigh thou for me.
    The broken heart is sadly free.

Aubrey de Vere, 'Lines'

From the storms of this world
    How gladly I'd fly,
To the calm of that breast,
    To the heaven of that eye!
How deeply I love thee
    'Twere useless to tell;
Farewell, then, my dear one,
    My Mary, farewell.

Jeremiah Joseph Callanan, 'Serenade'

first love is only a little foolishness and a lot of curiosity.

George Bernard Shaw as quoted by Des MacHale

Sweetheart of my life! –
As then, so now; nay, dearer to me now,
Since love, that fills the soul, expands it too,
And thus it holds more love, and ever more, –
O sweetheart, helpmate, guardian, better self!

William Allingham, 'George Levison or, The Schoolfellows'

"You gave me the key of your heart, my love;
    Then why do you make me knock?"
"Oh, that was yesterday, Saints above!
    And last night – I changed the lock!"

John Boyle O'Reilly, 'Constancy'

O Edain, wilt thou come with me
    To a wonderful palace that is mine?
    White are the teeth there, and black the brows,
    And crimson as the mead are the lips of the lovers.
    O woman, if thou comest to my proud people,
    'Tis a golden crown shall circle thy head,
    Thou shalt dwell by the sweet streams of my land,
    And drink of the mead and wine in the arms of thy
      lover.

Lady Wilde, 'Edain the Queen'

Dry be that tear, my gentlest love,
    Be hushed that struggling sigh:
Nor seasons, day, nor fate shall prove
    More fixed, more true, than I:
Hushed be that sigh, be dry that tear,
Cease boding doubt, cease anxious fear –
    Dry be that tear.

Richard Brinsley Sheridan, 'Dry Be That Tear'

Love is the sacrament of life; it sets
 Virtue where virtue was not; cleanses men
 Of all the vile pollutions of this world;
 It is the fire which purges gold from dross,
 It is the spring which in some wintry soil
 Makes innocence to blossom like a rose.

      Oscar Wilde, THE DUCHESS OF PADUA

Put your head, darling, darling, darling,
 Your darling black head my heart above;
 Oh, mouth of honey, with the thyme for fragrance,
 Who, with heart in breast, could deny you love?

   Anonymous, 'Dear Dark Head' (trans. Samuel Ferguson)

I do not love you as I loved
 The loves I have loved –
 As I may love others:

I know you are not beautiful
 As some I loved were beautiful –
 As others may be:

I do not hold your counsel dear
 As I've held others'
 As I still hold some:

And yet
 There is no truth but you
 No beauty but you
 No love but you –

And oh, there is no pain
 But you and me.

      Thomas MacGreevy, 'Dechtire'

At the mid hour of night, when stars are weeping, I fly
    To the lone vale we lov'd, when life shone warm in
        thine eye;
        And I think oft, if spirits can steal from the
            regions of air,
        To revisit past scenes of delight, thou wilt come to
            me there,
    And tell me our love is remember'd, even in the sky.

Thomas Moore, 'At the Mid Hour of Night'

I cannot hear his footstep, but it falls on my heart; he is beyond my senses, but love, that heavenly essence, gives me a feeling finer than sense, and I know that my lover comes; 'tis the air he breathes that conveys his presence to me, as it flutters through my heart.

Dion Boucicault, JESSIE BROWN

Great love of a man from another land
    Has come to me beyond all else:
    It has taken my bloom, no colour is left,
    It does not let me rest.

Anonymous, 'The Song of Crede, Daughter of Guare' (trans. Kuno Meyer)

You remember that evening
    We spent both together,
    'Neath the red-berried Rowan
    In still snowy weather.
Your white throat was singing,
    Your head on my shoulder –
Ne'er thought I, that evening,
    That love could grow colder.

'You Remember that Evening', a peasant ballad (trans. George Sigerson)

I know not night from day,
   Nor thrush from cuckoo gray,
Nor cloud from the sun that shines above thee –
   Nor freezing cold from heat,
   Nor friend – if friend I meet –
I but know – heart's love! – I love thee.

   Love that my Life began,
   Love, that will close life's span,
Love that grows ever by love-giving:
   Love, from the first to last,
   Love, till all life be passed,
Love that loves on after living!

Diarmad O'Curnain, 'Love's Despair' (trans. George Sigerson)

I'd cross the salt sea with you,
   Eivlin a rúin! [O secret treasure!]
And ne'er – ne'er I'd flee from you,
   Eivlin a rúin!
What soft tales I'd tell to you,
   I'd taste your lips' sweetness, too,
I'd sing 'mid the falling dew,
    "Eivlin a rúin!"

O! joy beyond life would bless, –
   Eivlin a rúin!
Should I wed your loveliness,
   Eivlin a rúin!
My fond arm would circle you,
My heart be your guardian true,
Ne'er maiden were loved like you,
   Eivlin a rúin!

Anonymous, 'Eivlin A Rúin' (trans. George Sigerson)

I through love have learned three things,
    Sorrow, sin, and death it brings;
    Yet day by day my heart within
    Dares shame and sorrow, death and sin:
    Maiden, you have aimed the dart
    Rankling in my ruined heart:
    Maiden, may the God above
    Grant you grace to grant me love!

Anonymous, 'The Fair-Haired Girl' (trans. Samuel Ferguson)

Sure if I were one of these flowers, and you were to pass me by like that, I do believe that I'd pluck myself and walk after you on my stalk.

    Dion Boucicault, THE SHAUGHRAUN

I sat with one I love last night,
    She sang to me an olden strain;
    In former times it woke delight,
        Last night – but pain.

Last night we saw the stars arise,
    But clouds soon dimmed the ether blue;
    And when we sought each other's eyes
        Tears dimmed them too!

We paced along our favorite walk,
    But paced in silence broken-hearted:
    Of old we used to smile and talk;
        Last night – we parted.

George Darley, 'Last Night'

The real genius for love lies not in getting into, but getting out of love.

    George Moore as quoted by Des MacHale

Canst thou be true to one alone,
　　True beyond all reproach –
　　Bound like the palmer to one goal,
　　Thrilled like the magnet by one pole –
　　　　Canst thou be such?

Charles Gavan Duffy, 'Love Song'

The red rose whispers of passion,
　　And the white rose breathes of love;
　　Oh, the red rose is a falcon,
　　　　And the white rose is a dove.

But I send you a cream-white rosebud
　　With a flush on its petal tips;
　　For the love that is purest and sweetest
　　　　Has a kiss of desire on the lips.

John Boyle O'Reilly, 'A White Rose'

Never give all the heart, for love
　　Will hardly seem worth thinking of
　　To passionate women if it seem
　　Certain, and they never dream
　　That it fades out from kiss to kiss;
　　For everything that's lovely is
　　But a brief, dreamy, kind delight.
　　O never give the heart outright,
　　For they, for all smooth lips can say,
　　Have given their hearts up to the play.
　　And who could play it well enough
　　If deaf and dumb and blind with love?
　　He that made this knows all the cost,
　　For he gave all his heart and lost.

W. B. Yeats, 'Never Give all the Heart'

She it is who stole my heart,
    And left a void and aching smart,
    But if she soften not her eye,
    I know that life and I must part.

Anonymous, 'My Love, Oh, She is My Love' (trans. Douglas Hyde)

Unfair, alas, the sharing
    that sorrow makes for lovers:
two hearts with but one owner,
    and no heart with another.

Maghnas O Domhnaill, Untitled (trans. Eleanor Knott)

family and nation

Your glass may be purple, and mine may be blue
    But, while they are filled from the same bright
        bowl
    The fool, who would quarrel for diff'rence of hue,
      Deserves not the comfort they shed o'er the soul.

Shall I ask the brave soldier who fights by my side
    In the cause of mankind, if our creeds agree?
    Shall I give up the friend I have valued and tried,
    If he kneel not before the same altar with me?

From the heretic girl of my soul should I fly,
    To seek somewhere else a more orthodox kiss?
    No: perish the hearts, and the laws that try
    Truth, valour, or love, by a standard like this!

Thomas Moore, 'Come, send round the wine'

I have not the courage to argue with my father.

Dion Boucicault, OLD HEADS AND YOUNG HEARTS

O brave young men, my love, my pride, my promise,
    'Tis on you my hopes are set,
  In manliness, in kindliness, in justice,
    To make Erin a nation yet;
  Self-respecting, self-relying, self-advancing,
    In union or in severance, free and strong,
  And if God grant this, then, under God, to Thomas
    Davis,
    Let the greater praise belong!

Samuel Ferguson, 'Lament for the Death of Thomas Davis'

true lovers of their country, can never be enemies to one half of their countrymen, or carry their resentment so far as to ruin the public for the sake of a party.

George Berkeley, 'An Essay Towards Preventing the Ruin of
Great Britain'

O faithful!
  Moulded in one womb,
  We two have stood together all the years,
  All the glad years and all the sorrowful years,
  Own brothers: through good repute and ill,
  In direct peril true to me,
  Leaving all things for me, spending yourself
  In the hard service that I taught to you,
  Of all the men that I have known on earth,
  You only have been my familiar friend,
  Nor needed I another.

Padraic Pearse, 'To My Brother'

there is no fireside like your own fireside.

An Irish proverb

All these ideals of freedom, of brotherhood, of power, of justice, of beauty, which have been at one time or another the fundamental idea in civilizations, are heaven-born, and descended from the divine world, incarnating first in the highest minds in each race, perceived by them and transmitted to their fellow-citizens; and it is the emergence or manifestation of one or other of these ideals in a group which is the beginning of a nation; and the more strongly the ideal is held the more powerful becomes the national being, because the synchronous vibration of many minds in harmony brings about almost unconsciously a psychic unity, a coalescing of the subconscious being of many. It is that inner unity which constitutes the national being.

A. E., 'The National Being'

These controversies, political, literary, and artistic, have showed that neither religion nor politics can of itself create minds with enough receptivity to become wise, or just and generous enough to make a nation. ... In Ireland I am constantly reminded of that fable of the futility of all discipline that is not of the whole being. Religious Ireland – and the pious Protestants of my childhood were signal examples – thinks of divine things as a round of duties separated from life and not as an element that may be discovered in all circumstance and emotion, while political Ireland sees the good citizen but as a man who holds to certain opinions and not as a man of good will. Against all this we have but a few educated men and the remnants of an old traditional culture among the poor. Both were stronger forty years ago, before the rise of our new middle class which made its first public display during the nine years of the Parnellite split, showing how base at moments of excitement are minds without culture.

W. B. Yeats, Notes to Collected Poems

nations act towards other nations as their own citizens act towards each other. ... If the citizens in any country could develop harmonious life among themselves they would manifest the friendliest feelings towards the people of other countries.

A. E., 'The National Being'

tradition gives depth to a man's mind. It gives him standards to judge by, to live up to. It gives him lineage, *noblesse*. It anchors him to a family, to a countryside, to a city, to a race. He will not drift with the tide like a piece of wreckage; he is attached to a ship that has ridden out many a storm and will ride out many more. His race lives in him; he thinks as they thought, their loyalties are his; his memory goes back to their beginnings; their long experience is his counsellor.

Fr Donnchadh Ó Floinn, STAR FOR IRISH YOUTH

You must show the landlords that you intend to keep a firm grip of your homesteads. ... You must help yourselves, and the public opinion of the world will stand by you and support you in your struggle to defend your homesteads.

Charles Stewart Parnell, speech at Westport, 8 June 1879

the true civilisation towards which by the grace of Heaven we are moving will not be based on this manufactured antagonism, but on a natural alliance. It will recognise that for the spirit, the mind and the body of man the country has its uses as well as the city. It will not desire to exalt one at the expense of the other, but letting each develop towards perfection in its own way, will draw its own character from the wealth of both.

George Townshend, THE GENIUS OF IRELAND

no nation, since the beginning of history, has ever drawn all its life out of itself.

W. B. Yeats, 'Samhain: 1904'

Be my epitaph writ on my country's mind
'He served his country and loved his kind'.

Thomas Davis as quoted by Smith O'Brien in 'The Nation in Mourning' by Lorna Kellett

the struggle for Irish freedom has two aspects: it is national and social. Its national ideal can never be realised until Ireland stands forth before the world a nation free and independent. It is social and economic, because no matter what the form of government may be, as long as one class owns as private property the land and instruments of labour from which all mankind derive their substance, that class will always have power to plunder and enslave the remainder of their fellow creatures. … The party which would lead the Irish people from bondage to freedom must then recognise both aspects of the long continued struggle of the Irish nation.

James Connolly in 1896, quoted in Socialism and Nationalism *(1948)*

mothers nursing their Children is a natural Duty.

Jonathan Swift, 'Mr. Collins's Discourse of Free-Thinking'

freedom is a condition which can be lost and won and lost again; nationality is a life which, if once lost, can never be recovered. A nation is a stubborn thing, very hard to kill; but a dead nation does not come back to life, any more than a dead man.

Padraic Pearse, 'The Spiritual Nation'

A man must consider his countrymen as God's creatures, and himself as accountable for his acting towards them.

George Berkeley, 'Maxims concerning Patriotism'

Whether you be a Protestant or Catholic, and whatever be your party, you will do well as an Irishman to ponder upon the spirit and principles which governed the public and private life of Grattan. Learn from him how to regard your countrymen of all denominations. Observe, as he did, how very much that is excellent belongs to both the great parties into which Ireland is divided. If (as some do) you entertain dispiriting views of Ireland, recollect that any country, containing such elements as those which roused the genius of Grattan, never need despair. *Sursum corda*. Be not disheartened.

Daniel Owen Madden, 'A Memoir of Henry Grattan'

It distresses me, O people steadfast,
  that with empty cravings you spurn your past
  save that age after age confirms the tale
  of the recovery of the Gael.

Gearóid Ó Clérigh, 'Reflection' (trans. by the author)

Beauty and truth

Her eyes they did shine like the diamonds,
   Her cheeks like the red rose in June.

   'The Maid with the Bonny Brown Hair', an Irish ballad

I am sick of the showy seeming
   Of a life that is half a lie;
   Of the faces lined with scheming
   In the throng that hurries by.
   From the sleepless thoughts' endeavour,
   I would go where the children play;
   For a dreamer lives forever,
   And a thinker dies in a day.

   John Boyle O'Reilly, 'The Cry of the Dreamer'

Deceit can make a man a fool, but not a coward.

   Dion Boucicault, JESSIE BROWN

'Greetings, Emer,' said Bricriu 'wife of the best warrior in Ulster. Emer of the Fair Hair is a proper name for you. All Erin's kings and princes contend for you in jealous rivalry. As the sun surpasses the stars of Heaven, you outshine the women of the whole world, in form and shape and birth, in youth and beauty and fame, in reputation and wisdom and speech.'

M. A. O'Brien, 'The Feast of Bricriu' quoted in FLED BRICRENN
(trans. by the author)

She comes to me like a star through the mist; her hair is golden and goes down to her shoes; her breast is the colour of white sugar, or like bleached bone on the card-table; her neck is whiter than the froth of the flood, or the swan coming from swimming. ... If France and Spain belonged to me, I'd give it up to be along with you.

Raftery, Untitled (trans. Lady Gregory)

She was lovely and fair as the rose of the summer,
Yet 'twas not her beauty alone that won me,
Oh, no, 'twas the truth in her eyes ever beaming
That made me love Mary, the Rose of Tralee.

William Pembroke Mulchinock, 'The Rose of Tralee'

Beauty, was, indeed, the cause of creation, since God made the world that He might provide the Angel of Beauty with a place where she might wander at will.

George Townshend, THE GENIUS OF IRELAND

A truth is a spiritual thing, a pure essence, whereas facts are concerned with matter.

Lord Dunsany, 'Three of the Arts' THE DONNELLAN LECTURES *1943*

The girl I love is comely, straight and tall,
    Down her white neck her auburn tresses fall,
    Her dress is neat, her carriage light and free –
    Here's a health to that charming maid whoe'er she be!

The rose's blush but fades beside her cheek,
    Her eyes are blue, her forehead pale and meek,
    Her lips like cherries on a summer tree –
    Here's a health to the charming maid whoe'er she be!

Jeremiah Joseph Callanan, 'The Girl I Love'

truth must be told, for the sake of the virtuous.

John Butler Yeats, letter to John Quinn, 6 November 1917

Her eyes like mountain water that's flowing on a rock,
    How clear they are, how dark they are! they give me
        many a shock;
    Red rowans warm in sunshine and wetted with a
        show'r,
    Could ne'er express the charming lip that has me in
        its pow'r.

Her nose is straight and handsome, her eyebrows lifted up,
    Her chin is very neat and pert, and smooth like a
        china cup.
    Her hair's the brag of Ireland, so weighty and so fine;
    It's rolling down upon her neck, and gather'd in a
        twine.

William Allingham, 'Lovely Mary Donnelly'

the licence of invention some people take is monstrous indeed.

Richard Brinsley Sheridan, THE SCHOOL FOR SCANDAL

truth makes us all akin.

George Townshend, The Genius of Ireland

> To be born woman is to know –
>> Although they do not talk of it at school –
>> That we must labour to be beautiful.

W. B. Yeats, 'Adam's Curse'

Be no tale-bearer, nor utterer of falsehoods; be not talkative nor rashly censorious. Stir not up strife against thee, however good a man thou be.

T. W. Rolleston, Myths and Legends of the Celtic Race

nothing in the world is more dangerous than truth to those who flout it.

Lord Dunsany, letter to Hazel Littlefield, 27 September 1955

> Away! the great life calls; I leave
>> For Beauty, Beauty's rarest flower;
>> For Truth, the lips that ne'er deceive;
>> For Love, I leave Love's haunted bower.

A. E., 'The Symbol Seduces'

truth is great and will prevail.

An Irish proverb

those truths which no Body can deny, will do no good to those who deny them.

Jonathan Swift, 'Mr. Collins's Discourse of Free-Thinking'

there was no part of Ireland I did not travel: from the rivers to the tops of the mountains, to the edge of Lough Greine, whose mouth is hidden; but I saw no beauty but was behind hers.

Her hair was shining, and her brows were shining too; her face was like herself, her mouth pleasant and sweet. She is the pride, and I give her the branch. She is the shining flower of Ballylee.

Raftery, 'Raftery's Praise of Mary Hynes' (trans. Lady Gregory)

every perception of beauty is vision with the divine eye, and not with the mortal sense.

A. E., 'Nationality and Imperialism'

'Tis the rose of the desert,
   So lovely so wild,
In the lap of the desert
   It's infancy smiled;
In the languish of beauty
   It droops o'er the thorn,
And its leaves are all wet
   With the bright tears of morn.
Yet 'tis better thou fair one,
   To dwell all alone,
Than recline on a bosom
   Less pure than thine own;
Thy form is too lovely
   To be torn from its stem,
And thy breath is too sweet
   For the children of men.

Jeremiah Joseph Callanan, 'Written to A Young Lady'

he who builds on lies rears only lies.
Padraic Pearse, 'Ghosts'

Be still as you are beautiful
  Be silent as the rose;
  Through miles of starlit countryside
  Unspoken worship flows
  To reach you in your loveless room
  From lonely men whom daylight gave
  The blessing of your passing face
  Impenetrably grave.

Patrick MacDonogh, 'Be Still as You Are Beautiful'

those who love beauty shall see beauty.

Edward Martyn, MAEVE

Where is the hand to trace
  The contour of her face:
  The nose so straight and fine
  Down from the forehead's line?

The curved and curtal lip
  Full in companionship
  With that lip's overplus,
  Proud and most sumptuous.

Oliver St John Gogarty, 'With a Coin from Syracuse'

One does not see anything until one sees its beauty. Then, and then only, does it come into existence.

Oscar Wilde, 'The Decay of Lying'

truth is not a thing of to-day or to-morrow. Beauty, heroism, and spirituality do not change like fashion, being the reflection of an unchanging spirit.

A. E., 'Literary Ideals in Ireland'

Beauty is Thought and Strength is Love.

James Stephens, THE CROCK OF GOLD

And her sweet red lips on these lips of mine
    Burned like the ruby fire set
In the swinging lamp of a crimson shrine,
    Or the bleeding wounds of the pomegranate,
    Or the heart of the lotus drenched and wet
With the spilt-out blood of the rose-red wine.

Oscar Wilde, 'In the Gold Room'

My eyes saw beauty itself,
    Like dashing spray in bright sunlight,
    When, caught, suddenly, by divinity,
    You danced.

And I knew love
    When my eyes met yours –
    Blessed eyes whose beatitude I may not see with.

For she is love itself to me for ever
    And beauty.
    But I,
    Because of absurdities,
    Must be content
    To cry to myself
    '*Thalassa!*'

Thomas MacGreevy, 'Ten Thousand Leaping Swords'

life and death

May you live as long as you want,
And never want as long as you live.

An Irish blessing

Work ... is the salt that gives flavour to life.

Dion Boucicault, THE OCTOROON

I wrote down my troubles every day;
And after a few short years,
When I turned to the heart-aches passed away,
I read them with smiles, not tears.

John Boyle O'Reilly, 'My Troubles!'

We are living on the physical plane; we are embodied spirits; and we must accept the conditions.

William Larminie, 'Legends as Material for Literature'

Everything changes:
   Time deranges
   Men and women and mountain ranges
   Why the Devil can't Time let Well enough alone?

Oliver St John Gogarty, 'The Dublin–Galway Train'

The young do not see death and the old see nothing else. ... In youth we don't see death. The stage is too crowded. In old age all the actors have left, and they were only actors, and death remains sitting patient on the stool.

John Butler Yeats, letter to W. B. Yeats, 17 July 1917

The life of the body's a cage,
   And the soul within it
Frets to escape, to be free,
   Like a lark or a linnet.
But since the struggle's in vain,
   She is weary ere long;
She chirps and she sings a little
   To assuage her wrong.

Katherine Tynan, 'The House of Life'

Which is, the Earth or the creatures that move upon it, the more important? This is a question prompted solely by intellectual arrogance, for in life there is no greater and no less. The thing that *is* has justified its own importance by mere existence, for that is the great and equal achievement. If life were arranged for us from without such a question of supremacy would assume importance, but life is always from within, and is modified or extended by our own appetites, aspirations, and central activities.

James Stephens, THE CROCK OF GOLD

Take time to work; it is the price of success.
Take time to think; it is the source of power.
Take time to play; it is the secret of perpetual youth.
Take time to read; it is the foundation of wisdom.
Take time to make friends; it is the road to happiness.
Take time to love and be loved; it is the privilege of
God.
Take time to share; life is too short to be selfish.
Take time to laugh; laughter is the music of God.

An Irish prayer

Death is a robber who heaps together kings, high princes and country lords; he brings with him the great, the young, and the wise, gripping them by the throat before all the people. Look at him who was yesterday swift and strong, who would leap stone wall, ditch and gap. Who was in the evening walking the street, and is going under the clay on the morrow.

Lady Gregory, KILTARTAN

Nature is cruel to living things. Rubies and crystals that do not feel are beautiful for ever, but flowers and women and artists fulfil their swift task of propagation and pass in a day.

J. M. Synge, 'Vita Vecchia'

When mine hour is come
Let no teardrop fall
And no darkness hover
Round me where I lie.
Let the vastness call
One who was its lover,
Let me breathe the sky.

A. E., 'When'

And sweet are all things, when we learn to prize them
  Not for their sake, but His who grants them or
  denies them.

Aubrey De Vere, 'Human Life'

Both your friend and your enemy think that you will never die.

An Irish proverb

no man at all can be living for ever, and we must be satisfied.

J. M. Synge, Riders to the Sea

God, on Whom Time never bears
  Disregard not mortal years,
  For a year to men may be
  Precious as eternity. ...

Leave them happy on the earth,
  Relative to death and birth
  Till, in peace, their minds transcend
  The Beginning and the End.

Oliver St John Gogarty, 'High Above Ohio'

Joys have three stages, Hoping, Having, and Had;
  The hands of Hope are empty, and the heart of
    Having is sad;
  For the joy we take, in the taking dies; and the joy we
    Had is its ghost.
  Now which is the better – the joy unknown, or the
    joy we have clasped and lost?

John Boyle O'Reilly, 'Yesterday and Tomorrow'

Death is not a mill-wheel you can stop at your will.

Lady Gregory, THE CANAVANS

Then sigh no more – if life is brief
So are its woes; and why repine?

James Clarence Mangan, 'Song'

there's no use for us trying to escape from fate.

Flann O'Brien, THE POOR MOUTH

God help the foolish sinner,
He always goes astray,
He rises up in the morning
But prays not with the day.
Mass he has long forsaken,
Forgotten how to pray,
Where shall he go when Death shall come
And he leaves the world for aye?

Anonymous, 'The Foolish Sinner' (trans. Douglas Hyde)

Destiny is sometimes profound, sometimes simple.

Lord Dunsany, 'Three of the Arts' THE DONNELLAN LECTURES *1943*

Our life should resemble a long day of light,
And our death come on holy and calm as the night!

Thomas Moore, 'Oh! Had We Some Bright Little Isle of Our Own!'

to each man his fate.

Dion Boucicault, JESSIE BROWN

the dead are never really dead ... until we cease to think of them.

George Moore, CELIBATE LIVES

Speak no more of life,
What can life bestow,
In this amphitheatre of strife,
All times dark with tragedy and woe?
Knowest thou not how care and pain
Build their lampless dwelling in the brain,
Ever, as the stern intrusion
Of our teachers, time and truth,
Turn to gloom the bright illusion,
Rainbowed on the soul of youth?
Could I live to find that this is so?
Oh! no! no!

James Clarence Mangan, 'The Dying Enthusiast'

the thought that our existence terminates with this life doth naturally check the soul in any generous pursuit, contract her views, and fix them on temporary and selfish ends. It dethrones the reason, extinguishes all noble and heroick sentiments, and subjects the mind to the slavery of every present passion.

George Berkeley, 'The Sanctions of Religion'

after great merriment comes sorrow and good weather never remains for ever.

Flann O'Brien, THE POOR MOUTH

Decay is the fate of every creature.

Daniél ua Líathaiti, 'Sell not Heaven for Sin' (trans. Gerard Murphy)

> A sunset's mounded cloud;
>   A diamond evening-star;
>   Sad blue hills afar;
>   Love in his shroud.
>
> Scarcely a tear to shed;
>   Hardly a word to say;
>   The end of a summer day;
>   Sweet Love dead.

William Allingham, 'An Evening'

Why do you speak of to-morrow while it is still to-day.

Edward Martyn, MAEVE

> The fight with Death is hard and long;
>   (Though Death is strong his pace is slow),
>   Like helpless ships we turn and toss
>   And drift across the waves of woe.

Anonymous, 'The Repentance of the Joyce from the County of Mayo, Close to Ballinrobe' (trans. Douglas Hyde)

> Solomon! where is thy throne? It is gone in the wind.
>   Babylon! where is thy might? It is gone in the wind.
>   All that the genius of Man hath achieved or designed
>   Waits but its hour to be dealt with as dust by the
>   wind.

James Clarence Mangan, 'Gone in the Wind'

We might as well just save our breath,
There's not a good word to be said for Death
Except for the great change it brings:
For who could bear the loveliest Springs
Touched by the thought that he must keep
A watch eternal without sleep?

Oliver St John Gogarty, 'Elegy on the Archpoet
William Butler Yeats, Lately Dead'

talk of misfortunes and misfortunes will come.

Lady Gregory, SPREADING THE NEWS

If I might choose where my tired limbs shall lie
When my task here is done, the oak's green crest
Shall rise above my grave – a little mound,
Raised in some cheerful village cemetery.
And I could wish, that, with unceasing sound,
A lonely mountain rill was murmuring by –
In music – through the long soft twilight hours.
And let the hand of her, whom I love best,
Plant round the bright green grave those fragrant
flowers
In whose deep bells the wild-bee loves to rest;
And should the robin from some neighbouring tree
Pour his enchanted song – oh! softly tread,
For sure, if aught of earth can soothe the dead,
He still must love that pensive melody!

John Anster, 'If I Might Choose'

you get what's coming to you, and if it doesn't come, why
worry?

Norah Hoult, MRS. JOHNSON

For what is death to him who dies
    With God's own blessing on his head?
A charter – not a sacrifice –
    A life immortal to the dead.
And life itself is only great
    When man devotes himself to be
By virtue, thought, and deed, the mate
    Of God's own children and the free.

George Phillips, 'Brothers, Arise!'

God has His scheme laid out for the human race, and every individual has a special ideal born of his own nature. But progress towards the ideal needs choice and effort. The human will should be exercised in making the decision and in then vigorously carrying it out, and even should failure be the result, the will should never falter nor faith be lost.

George Townshend, THE GENIUS OF IRELAND

Why do you tear from me my darling son,
    The fruit of my womb?
It was I who bore him,
My breast he drank.
My womb carried him about,
My vitals he sucked,
My heart he filled.
He was my life,
'Tis death to have him taken from me.
My strength has ebbed,
My speech is silenced,
My eyes are blinded.

Anonymous, 'The Mothers' Lament at the Slaughter of the Innocents'
(trans. Kuno Meyer)

ah! sure the future belongs to Heaven, but the present is our own.

Dion Boucicault, THE SHAUGHRAUN

> To die is soon or late
> For every being born alive
> the equal doom of Fate.

Samuel Ferguson, 'Congal Claen: The Warnings Given Him'

the man dies, but his memory lives.

Robert Emmet, speech from the dock

Birth into mortality is but a sleep and a forgetting.

George Townshend, THE GENIUS OF IRELAND

> May your thoughts be as glad as the shamrocks.
> May your heart be as light as a song.
> May each day bring you bright happy hours,
> That stay with you all year long.
> For each petal on the shamrock
> This brings a wish your way –
> Good health, good luck, and happiness
> For today and every day.

An Irish blessing

> Death's but a pass that must be trod,
> If man would ever pass to God:
> A port of calms, a state of ease
> From the rough rage of swelling seas.

Thomas Parnell, From 'Night Piece on Death'

Perhaps when I am gone the thought of me
    May sometimes be your acceptable guest.
    Indeed you love me: but my company
    Old time makes tedious; and to part is best.
    Not without Nature's will are natures wed:–
    O gentle Death, how dear thou makest the dead!

Aubrey de Vere, 'Incompatibility'

Let fate do her worst, there are relics of joy,
    Bright dreams of the past, which she cannot destroy;
    And which come, in the night-time of sorrow and
        care,
    To bring back the features that joy used to wear.
    Long, long be my heart with such memories fill'd!
    Like the vase in which roses have once been distill'd –
    You may break, you may ruin the vase, if you will,
    But the scent of the roses will hang round it still.

Thomas Moore, 'Farewell! But Whenever You Welcome the Hour'

Cast a cold eye
    On life, on death.
    Horseman, pass by!

W. B. Yeats, 'Under Ben Bulben'

forging a nation

leadership and liberty

THE PROCLAMATION OF THE IRISH REPUBLIC
Easter 1916

* * *

POBLACHT NA HEIREANN
The Provisional Government of the Irish Republic
To the People of Ireland.

IRISHMEN AND IRISHWOMEN: In the name of God and of the dead generations from which she receives her old tradition of nationhood, Ireland, through us, summons her children to her flag and strikes for her freedom.

Having organised and trained her manhood through her secret revolutionary organisation, the Irish Republican Brotherhood, and through her open military organisations, the Irish Volunteers and the Irish Citizen Army, having patiently perfected her discipline, having resolutely waited for the right moment to reveal itself, she now seizes that moment, and, supported by her exiled children in America and by gallant allies in Europe, but relying in the first on her own strength, she strikes in full confidence of victory.

We declare the right of the people of Ireland to the ownership of Ireland, and to the unfettered control of Irish destinies, to be sovereign and indefeasible. The long usurpation of that right by a foreign people and government has not extinguished the right, nor can it ever be extinguished except by the destruction of the Irish people. In every generation the Irish people have asserted their right to national freedom and sovereignty; six times during the past three hundred years they have asserted it in arms. Standing on that fundamental right and again asserting it in arms in the face of the world, we hereby proclaim the Irish Republic as a Sovereign Independent State, and we pledge our lives and the lives of our comrades-in-arms to the cause of its freedom, of its welfare, and of its exaltation among the nations.

The Irish Republic is entitled to, and hereby claims, the allegiance of every Irishman and Irishwoman. The Republic guarantees religious and civil liberty, equal rights and equal opportunities to all its citizens, and declares its resolve to pursue the happiness and prosperity of the whole nation and of all its parts, cherishing all the children of the nation equally, and oblivious of the differences carefully fostered by an alien government, which have divided a minority from the majority in the past.

Until our arms have brought the opportune moment for the establishment of a permanent National Government, representative of the whole people of Ireland and elected by the suffrages of all her men and women, the Provisional Government, hereby constituted, will administer the civil and military affairs of the Republic in trust for the people.

We place the cause of the Irish Republic under the protection of the Most High God, Whose blessing we invoke upon our arms, and we pray that no one who serves that cause will dishonour it by cowardice, inhumanity, or rapine. In this supreme hour the Irish nation must, by its valour and discipline and by the readiness of its children to sacrifice themselves for the common good, prove itself worthy of the august destiny to which it is called.

Signed on Behalf of the Provisional Government,

THOMAS J. CLARKE,

SEAN MacDIARMADA, THOMAS MacDONAGH,
P. H. PEARSE, EAMONN CEANNT,
JAMES CONNOLLY. JOSEPH PLUNKETT.

When once man goes out of his sphere, and says he will legislate for God, he, in fact, makes himself God.

Henry Grattan, speech on the injustice of disqualification of
Catholics, 31 May 1811

A man who can only talk common-place, and act according to routine, has little weight. To speak, look, and do what your own soul from its depths orders you, are credentials of greatness which all men understand and acknowledge. ... Such men are the pioneers of civilization, and the rulers of the human heart.

Thomas Davis, 'Our National Language', THE NATION, *1 April 1843*

In deed exalted, humble in thy pride,
    Most firm when lowering dangers thee betide;
    Son of my soul, be then thy spirit prov'd
    And in the battle's rage persist unmov'd
    Ne'er free submission to thy will restrain,
    And, strict, thy just prerogatives maintain:
    To man of violence entrust no pow'r,
    Or else thy country rues the fatal hour;
    For know, O! King, disorder oft proceeds
    From such subord'nate man's inord'nate deeds.

Mac Bruaideaha, 'Advice to King O'Brien'
(trans. Theophilus O'Flanagan)

nations are not primarily ruled by laws: less by violence.

Edmund Burke, 'Thoughts on the Cause of the Present Discontents, 1770'

Of him who found his country
> Down-stricken, gagged, and chained;
Who, battling still, untired, unawed,
From triumph on to triumph trod,
> In bloodless warfare gained.
Peace was his idol – truth his sword.

Sliabh Cuilinn, 'The Thirtieth of May'

there are things a man must not do to save a nation.

John O' Leary as quoted by W. B. Yeats in 'Poetry and Tradition'

But we know the *Liberties* of Englishmen are Founded on that Universal *Law of Nature*, that ought to prevail throughout the whole World, *of being Govern'd only by such Laws to which they give their own Consent by their Representatives in Parliament.*

THE MAGNA CARTA HIBERNIAE *quoted by William Molyneux in* THE CASE OF IRELAND

In battle meddle not with a buffoon, for … he is but a fool.

T. W. Rolleston, MYTHS AND LEGENDS OF THE CELTIC RACE

the country that condescends either to bully or to permit itself to be bullied soon ceases to have any fine qualities.

W. B. Yeats, public statement, 29 January 1907

men are apt to measure national prosperity by riches. It would be righter to measure it by the use that is made of them.

*George Berkeley, 'An Essay Towards Preventing the
Ruin of Great Britain'*

From the time I could observe and reflect, I perceived that there were two kinds of laws – the laws of the state and the laws of God – frequently clashing with each other. By the latter kind, I have always endeavoured to regulate my conduct; but that laws of the former kind do exist in Ireland I believe no one who hears me can deny. That such laws have existed in former times many and various examples clearly evince.

Thomas Russell, speech from the dock

> *To* place and power all public spirit tends,
>   *In* place and power all public spirit ends;
>   Like hardy plants, that love the air and sky,
>   When *out*, 'twill thrive – but taken *in*, 'twill die!

Thomas Moore, 'Corruption: An Epistle'

Public life is a situation of power and energy; he trespasses against his duty who sleeps upon his watch, as well as he that goes over to the enemy.

*Edmund Burke, 'Thoughts on the Cause of the Present
Discontents, 1770'*

I have but one religion, the old Persian: to bend the bow and tell the truth.

John O' Leary as quoted by W. B. Yeats in 'Poetry and Tradition'

Concord and union among ourselves is rather to be hoped for as an effect of public spirit than proposed as a means to promote it.

George Berkeley, 'An Essay Towards Preventing the
Ruin of Great Britain'

In peace or in war
    Dwell not afar
From the voice of thy people, nor hide
Thy heart in the purple of pride;
    Bend down thine ear,
Let the doors to thy mansion be wide,
    Let the pathway be clear
    So that all thou shalt hear,
And the injured shall come to thy side.

Anonymous, 'The King's Lay' (trans. George Sigerson)

The temper of the people amongst whom he presides ought therefore to be the first study of a statesman. And the knowledge of this temper it is by no means impossible for him to attain, if he has not an interest in being ignorant of what it is his duty to learn.

Edmund Burke, 'Thoughts on the Cause of the Present
Discontents, 1770'

Nations hate other nations for the evil which is in themselves; but they are as little given to self-analysis as individuals, and while they are right to overcome evil, they should first try to understand the genesis of the passion in their own nature. If we understand this, many of the ironies of history will be intelligible.

A. E., 'The National Being'

The proper aim is to try and reconstruct society on such a basis that poverty will be impossible.

Oscar Wilde, 'The Soul of Man'

Be not too wise, nor too foolish,
    be not too conceited, nor too diffident,
    be not too haughty, nor too humble,
    be not too talkative, nor too silent,
    be not too hard, nor too feeble.

If you be too wise, one will expect too much of you;
    if you be too foolish, you will be deceived;
    if you be too conceited, you will be thought vexatious;
    if you be too humble, you will be without honour;
    if you be too talkative, you will not be heeded;
    if you be too silent, you will not be regarded;
    if you be too hard, you will be broken;
    if you be too feeble, you will be crushed.

Anonymous, 'Instructions of King Cormac' (trans. Kuno Meyer)

No power is given for the sole sake of the holder; and although government certainly is an institution of divine authority, yet its forms, and the persons who administer it, all originate from the people.

Edmund Burke, 'Thoughts on the Cause of the Present Discontents, 1770'

I have laboured to create a people in Ireland by raising three millions of my countrymen to the rank of citizens. I have laboured to abolish the infernal spirit of religious persecution, by uniting the Catholics and Dissenters.

Wolfe Tone, speech from the dock

The man of fame who influences thousands, cannot often command the confidence of his nearest and dearest.

Edward Martyn, THE TALE OF A TOWN

But let me ask you if you have forgotten what was the faith of your ancestors, or if you are prepared to assert that the men who procured your liberties are unfit to make your laws?

Henry Grattan, speech on the injustice of disqualification of Catholics, 31 May 1811

'O grandson of Con, O Cormac,' said Cairbré, 'what is good for a king.'

'That is plain,' said Cormac, 'it is good for him to have patience and not to dispute, self-government without anger, affability without haughtiness, diligent attention to history, strict observance of covenants and agreements, strictness mitigated by mercy in the execution of laws. ...'

'O grandson of Con, O Cormac,' said Cairbré, 'what is good for the welfare of a country?'

'That is plain,' said Cormac, 'frequent convocations of sapient and good men to investigate its affairs, to abolish each evil and retain each wholesome institution, to attend to the precepts of the elders; let every assembly be convened according to law, let the law be in the hands of the nobles, let the chieftains be upright and unwilling to oppress the poor.'

Attributed to King Cormac, 'The Instruction of a Prince'
(trans. Douglas Hyde)

Government is a contrivance of human wisdom to provide for human *wants*.

Edmund Burke, 'Reflections on the Revolution in France, 1790'

No form of government we know is perfect, and none will be permanent.

A. E., 'Nationality and Imperialism'

Each succeeding generation of your countrymen have deplored the unwisdom of their predecessors and themselves fallen into the very errors they condemned. Ought you not to make sure that you avoid doing likewise...?

Eamon de Valera, letter to Anthony Eden, 1939

In reality there are two, and only two, foundations of law .... equity and utility.

Edmund Burke, 'Tract on the Popery Laws'

But it so happens, and it will ever happen so, that they who have lived to serve their country – no matter how weak their efforts may have been – are sure to receive the thanks and blessings of its people.

Thomas Francis Meagher, speech from the dock

Arbitrary power is a thing which neither any man can hold nor any man can give. No man can lawfully govern himself according to his own will; much less can one person be governed by the will of another.

Edmund Burke, 'Speeches on the Impeachment of Warren Hastings, 15 February 1788'

fReeÒom anÒ justice

freedom is a thing that you cannot cut in two – you are either all free or you are not free.

Eamon de Valera, IRISH INDEPENDENT, *6 December 1921*

To the Irish mind for more than a thousand years freedom has had but one definition. It has meant not a limited freedom, a freedom conditioned by the interests of another nation, a freedom compatible with the suzerain authority of a foreign parliament, but absolute freedom, the sovereign control of Irish destinies. It has meant not the freedom of a class, but the freedom of a people. It has meant not the freedom of a geographical fragment of Ireland, but the freedom of all Ireland, of every sod of Ireland.

And the freedom thus defined has seemed to the Irish the most desirable of all earthly things. They have valued it more than land, more than wealth, more than ease, more than empire.

Padraic Pearse, 'Ghosts'

how can a man *think* at all, if he does not think freely?

Jonathan Swift, 'Mr. Collins's Discourse of Free-Thinking'

History's lessons, if thou read 'em,
   All proclaim this truth to thee:
  Knowledge is the price of freedom –
   Know thyself, and thou art free!
Know, oh! man, thy proud vocation –
   Stand erect, with calm, clear brow –
Happy! happy, were our nation
   If thou hadst that knowledge now!

D. F. MacCarthy, 'The Price of Freedom'

I hope that it may not be necessary for us in the new Parliament to devote our attention to subsidiary measures, and that it may be possible for us to have a programme and a platform with only one plank, and that one plank National Independence.

Charles Stewart Parnell, speech on Home Rule, 24 August 1885

my political creed is short and simple. It consists in believing that all men are entitled as of right and justice to religious and civil liberty. ... [Religion] is debased and degraded by human interference; and surely the worship of the Deity cannot but be contaminated by the admixture of worldly ambition or human force.

Daniel O'Connell, speech at Tralee, County Kerry, 1818

Successful revolutions are not the product of our brains, but of ripe material conditions.

James Connolly, 'Labour in Irish History', 1910

freedom was never won by murder, for heaven never yet armed the hand of an assassin.

Dion Boucicault, Jessie Brown

Oh! the French are on the sea,
    Says the *shan van vocht*;
The French are on the sea,
    Says the *shan van vocht*:
Oh! the French are in the Bay,
They'll be here without delay,
And the Orange will decay,
    Says the *shan van vocht*…

Yes! Ireland shall be free,
    From the centre to the sea;
    Then hurrah for Liberty!
        Says the *shan van vocht*.
    Chorus
            Yes! Ireland shall be free,
            From the centre to the sea:
            Then hurrah for Liberty!
Says the *shan van vocht*.

'The Shan Van Vocht', street ballad, 1797

God gave to me a mind that is my own, a mind that has not been mortgaged to the opinion of any man or set of men, a mind that I was to use and not surrender.

Thomas Francis Meagher, speech from the dock

Irishmen, I call on you to join in crushing slavery and in giving liberty to every man of every caste, creed and color.

Daniel O'Connell, address to the Repeal Association, 1843

The British minister mistakes the Irish character; had he intended to make Ireland a slave, he should have kept her a beggar; there is no middle policy; win her heart by the restoration of her right, or cut off the nation's right hand; greatly emancipate, or fundamentally destroy. We may talk plausibly to England, but so long as she exercises a power to bind this country, so long are the nations in a state of war; the claims of the one go against the liberty of the other, and the sentiments of the latter go to oppose those claims to the last drop of her blood. The English opposition, therefore, are right; mere trade will not satisfy Ireland:– they judge of us by other great nations, by the nation whose political life has been a struggle for liberty; they judge of us with a true knowledge, and just deference, for our character: that a country enlightened as Ireland, chartered as Ireland, armed as Ireland, and injured as Ireland, will be satisfied with nothing less than liberty.

Henry Grattan quoted by Thomas Davis in 'Speeches of Grattan'

Is not freedom as necessary as love to my human soul or to any people? Can there be any real brotherhood without it? If we are debarred from the freedom we would have, how narrow is the range for human effort!

A. E., 'Nationality and Imperialism'

I entirely agree with you on the principle of freedom of conscience, and no man can admit that sacred principle without extending it equally to the Jew as to the Christian. To my mind it is an eternal and universal truth that we are responsible to God alone for our religious belief and that human laws are impious when they attempt to control the exercise of those acts of individual or general devotion which such belief requires.

Daniel O'Connell, letter to Isaac Lyon Goldsmid, 1829

I had rather be a slave with a free soul than remain free with a slavish, deceitful heart.

Dion Boucicault, THE OCTOROON

Liberty is the greatest human blessing that a virtuous man can possess.

George Berkeley, 'An Essay Towards Preventing the Ruin of Great Britain'

> Oh, Freedom! once thy flame hath fled
> It never lights again.

Thomas Moore, 'Weep on, weep on'

There was sorrow on his father then, and he said: "What was it drove you out of the country you were king over?" And Bres said: "Nothing drove me out but my own injustice and my own hardness; I took away their treasures from the people, and their jewels, and their food itself. And there were never taxes put on them before I was their king."

"That is bad," said his father; "it is of their prosperity you had a right to think more than of your own kingship. And their good-will would be better than their curses," he said; "and what is it you are come to look for here?" "I am come to look for fighting men," said Bres, "that I may take Ireland by force." "You have no right to get it by injustice when you could not keep it by justice," said his father.

Lady Gregory, GODS AND FIGHTING MEN

We are in a Miserable Condition indeed, if we may not be allow'd to Complain, when we think we are Hurt; and to give our Reasons with all Modesty and Submission.

William Molyneux, THE CASE OF IRELAND

We must be strong and self-sacrificing and ready to sink all our feelings of class and other differences in a firm resolve to unite for obtaining our just rights.

Edward Martyn, The Tale of a Town

Were treachery, falsehood, and disloyalty left unpunished, society must become like an arena full of wild beasts, tearing one another to pieces.

George Bernard Shaw, Cæsar and Cleopatra

No rising column marks this spot
    Where many a victim lies;
  But oh! the blood which here has streamed
    To Heaven for justice cries.

It claims it on the oppressor's head
    Who joys in human woe,
  Who drinks the tears by misery shed,
    And mocks them as they flow ...

It claims it for his ruined isle,
    Her wretched children's grave;
  Where withered Freedom droops her head,
    And man exists – a slave!

Robert Emmet, lines dedicated to Arbour Hill

The most dangerous war is that which has its origin in just claims denied or in a clash of opposing rights – and not merely opposing interests – when each side can see no reason in justice why it should yield its claim to the other.

Eamon de Valera, broadcast to America from Geneva, 1938

I know no human being exempt from the law. The law is the security of … every person that is governed, and of every person that governs.

Edmund Burke, 'Speech in General Reply to the Evidence called on behalf of Warren Hastings: First Day: 28 May 1794'

It is idle to look for peace between nations or domestic peace within a nation, except on a foundation of justice.

Eamon de Valera, statement made in Belfast, 22 June 1922

BRAVERY AND COURAGE

Does the sentence of death, which your unhallowed policy inflicts on my body, condemn my tongue to silence and my reputation to reproach? Your executioner may abridge the period of my existence, but while I exist I shall not forbear to vindicate my character and motives from your aspersions; and, as a man to whom fame is dearer than life, I will make the last use of that life in doing justice to that reputation which is to live after me, and which is the only legacy I can leave to those I honour and love, and for whom I am proud to perish.

Robert Emmet, speech from the dock

War is the profession of the princes of whom it treats, a type of war which is direct and straightforward, almost devoid of strategy, and commonly decided by the personal prowess of leaders.

Gerard Murphy, SAGA AND MYTH IN ANCIENT IRELAND

every heroic deed is an act of the spirit.

A. E., 'Nationality and Imperialism'

When Pezar fights and shakes his dreadful spear,
　　Whole armies fly and heroes quake with fear:
　　What shielded foe, what champion can withstand,
　　The blazing spear in mighty Pezar's hand!

P. W. Joyce, OLD CELTIC ROMANCES

then Lugaid threw the spear, and it went through and through
Cuchulain's body, and he knew he had got his deadly wound
… his only horse went away from him … and left his master, the
king of the heroes of Ireland, to die upon the plain of
Muirthemne. …

There was a pillar-stone west of the lake, and his eye lit on it,
and he went to the pillar-stone, and [Cuchulain] tied himself to
it with his breast-belt, the way he would not meet his death lying
down, but would meet it standing up.

Lady Gregory, CUCHULAIN OF MUIRTHEMNE

Just by the strength of their hands
　　The Fenians' battles were fought,
　　With never a spoken lie,
　　Never a lie in thought. …

If happier house than Heaven
　　There be, above or below,
　　'Tis there my master Fionn
　　And his fighting men will go.

Anonymous, 'The Praise of Fionn' (trans. Frank O'Connor)

We drink the memory of the brave,
The faithful and the few:
Some lie far off beyond the wave,
Some sleep in Ireland, too;
All, all are gone; but still lives on
The fame of those who died;
All true men, like you, men,
Remember them with pride.

John Kells Ingram, 'The Memory of the Dead' (1798)

Courage – your most necessary virtue – consists not in blind resistance, but in knowing when to forbear.

THE NATION, *17 June 1843*

In Mountjoy on Monday morning,
High upon the gallows tree,
Kevin Barry gave his young life
For the cause of Liberty.
But a lad of eighteen summers,
Yet no one can deny,
As he walked to death that morning
He proudly held his head on high. ...

Calmly standing to 'attention',
While he bade his last farewell
To his broken-hearted mother,
Whose grief no one can tell.
For the cause he proudly cherished
This sad parting had to be,
Then to death walked softly smiling,
That old Ireland might be free.

'Kevin Barry', Broadsheet Ballad

The Minstrel Boy to the war is gone,
    In the ranks of the dead you'll find him;
    His father's sword he has girded on,
    And his wild harp slung behind him.
    'Land of song', said the warrior bard,
    'Though all the world betray thee,
    One sword, at least, thy rights shall guard,
    One faithful harp shall praise thee.'

The Minstrel fell – but the foeman's chain
    Could not bring his proud soul under;
    The harp he lov'd ne'er spoke again,
    For he tore its chords asunder;
    And said, 'No chains shall sully thee,
    Thou soul of love and bravery.
    Thy songs were made for the pure and free,
    They shall never sound in slavery.'

Thomas Moore, 'The Minstrel Boy'

politics and nationalism

A good Nationalist is, I suppose, one who is ready to give up a great deal that he may preserve to his country whatever part of her possessions he is best fitted to guard.

W. B. Yeats, 'Samhain: 1903'

I f we wish to become a self-respecting, self-relying, and really independent nation we must have minds of our own. We must be ourselves.

UNITED IRELAND, *4 June 1892*

A Resurrection! Aye, out of the grave of the first Irishman or woman murdered for protesting against Ireland's participation in this thrice accursed war will arise anew the Spirit of the Irish Revolution. ... If you strike at, imprison or kill us, out of our graves we will evoke a spirit that will thwart you and, mayhap, raise a force that will destroy you.

James Connolly, in IRISH WORK, *19 December 1914*

What makes religious questions loom large in Ireland? Is it the main lines of political division happen to coincide with the religious ones?

Eamon de Valera quoted in CHRISTIAN SCIENCE MONITOR,
15 May 1918

We defeated Conscription in spite of their threats,
 And we're going to defeat ould Lloyd-George and his
  pets;
 For Ireland and freedom we're here to a man,
 And we'll humble the pride of the bould Black and
  Tan.

'The Bould Black and Tan', an Irish ballad

Ireland is in your hands, in your power. If you do not save her, she cannot save herself. I solemnly call on you to recollect that I predict with the sincerest conviction that a quarter of her population will perish unless you come to her relief.

Daniel O'Connell, debate on the Soup Kitchen Act

England's difficulty is Ireland's opportunity.

Political slogan

I was but a little child with my little book going to school, and by the house there I saw the agent. He took the unfortunate tenant and thrun him in the road, and I saw the man's wife come out crying and the agent's wife thrun her in the channel, and when I saw that, though I was but a child, I swore I'd be a Nationalist. I swore by heaven, and I swore by hell and all the rivers that run through there.

A local politician quoted by Jack Yeats in 'With Synge in Connemara,' 1911

No man has the right to fix the boundary of the march of a nation; no man has a right to say to his country – thus far shalt thou go and no further.

Charles Stewart Parnell, speech at Cork, 21 January 1885

The literary man, who is, or ought to be, concerned mainly with intellectual interests, should only intervene in politics when principles affecting the spiritual life of his country are involved.

A. E., 'Nationality and Imperialism'

Political problems do not primarily concern truth or false-hood. They relate to good or evil. What in the result is likely to produce evil is politically false; that which is productive of good, politically true.

Edmund Burke, 'Letter from the New to the Old Whigs, 1791'

The Bishops and the Party
    That tragic story made,
    A husband that had sold his wife
    And after that betrayed;
    But stories that live longest
    Are sung above the glass,
    And Parnell loved his country,
    And Parnell loved his lass.

W. B. Yeats, 'Come Gather Round Me, Parnellites'

One can serve one's country alone out of the abundance of one's own heart, and it is labour enough to be certain one is in the right, without having to be certain that one's thought is expedient also.

W. B. Yeats, 'Samhain: 1903'

An Irishman's first duty is to his country, his second is to his King, and both are now, and by God's blessing will, I hope, remain, united and inseparable.

Wolfe Tone, 'An Argument on Behalf of the Catholics of Ireland' (1791)

Realities are too strong, party passions too violent to bear to see, or care to look at their faces in the looking-glass. The people would only break the glass, and curse the fool who held the mirror up to nature – distorted nature, in a fever.

Maria Edgeworth, letter to M. Pakenham Edgeworth, Esq., 19 February 1834

Irish nationality is an ancient spiritual tradition, and the Irish nation could not die as long as that tradition lived in the heart of one faithful man or woman.

Padraic Pearse, 'The Spiritual Nation'

Soon after I had relinquished the Kingdom of God I began to take a real interest in the kingdom of Ireland. My politics went round from a vigorous and unreasoning loyalty to a temperate Nationalism. Everything Irish became sacred ... and had a charm that was neither quite human nor divine, rather perhaps as if I had fallen in love with a goddess, although I had still sense enough not to personify Erin in the patriotic verse I now sought to fabricate. Patriotism gratifies Man's need for adoration and has therefore a peculiar power upon the imaginative sceptic, as we see in France at the present time.

J. M. Synge, 'Autobiography'

No one has the right to limit the aspirations of a people.

Charles Stewart Parnell as quoted by Katharine O'Shea

my country was my idol. To it I sacrificed every selfish, every endearing sentiment; and for it I now offer up myself, O God! No, my lords; I acted as an Irishman determined on delivering my country from the yoke of a foreign and unrelenting tyranny and the more galling yoke of a domestic faction, which is its joint partner and perpetrator in the patricide, from the ignominy existing with an exterior of splendour and a conscious depravity. It was the wish of my heart to extricate my country from this doubly riveted despotism – I wished to place her independence beyond the reach of any power on earth. I wished to exalt her to that proud station in the world.

Robert Emmet, speech from the dock

O! the Erne shall run red
    With redundance of blood,
The earth shall rock beneath our tread,
    And flames wrap hill and wood,
And gun-peal, and slogan cry
    Wake many a glen serene,
Ere you shall fade, ere you shall die,
    My Dark Rosaleen!
    My own Rosaleen!
The Judgment Hour must first be nigh,
Ere you can fade, ere you can die,
    My Dark Rosaleen!

James Clarence Mangan, 'Dark Rosaleen' (trans. by the author)

meanwhile, even as a partitioned small nation, we shall go on and strive to play our part in the world continuing unswervingly to work for the cause of true freedom and for peace and understanding.

Eamon de Valera, public reply to Winston Churchill, 16 May 1945

What has occasioned the failure of the cause is useless to speculate on – Providence orders all things for the best. *I am sure the people will never abandon the cause; I am equally sure it will succeed.* I trust men will see, that the only true basis of liberty is morality and the only stable basis of morality is religion.

Thomas Russell, speech from the dock

To partition the territory of an ancient nation is one of the cruellest wrongs that can be committed against a people. The partition of Ireland is in essence not different from the partition of Poland, nor are the evils of it less in kind than those which Abraham Lincoln foresaw from the projected partition of the United States.

Eamon de Valera, from a statement in 1942, quoted in
Fianna Fáil: The Story of Fianna Fáil

two *wee girls*
  were playing tig near a car …

how many counties would you say
  are worth their scattered fingers?

Desmond Egan, 'The Northern Ireland Question'

Ireland has been knocking at the English door long enough with kid gloves, and now she will knock with a mailed hand.

Charles Parnell, speech in private during 1885 election at Liverpool, recalled in Tuam Herald *obituary by William O'Malley*

When my country takes her place among the nations of the earth, *then, and not till then*, let my epitaph be written. I have done.

Robert Emmet, speech from the dock

Ireland must exchange the patriotism which looks back for the patriotism which looks forward.

John Eglinton, 'What Should be the Subjects of a National Drama?'

epilogue

Begin again to the summoning birds
   to the sight of light at the window,
   begin to the roar of morning traffic
   all along Pembroke Road.
   Every beginning is a promise
   born in light and dying in dark
   determination and exaltation of springtime
   flowering the way to work.
   Begin to the pageant of queuing girls
   the arrogant loneliness of swans in the canal
   bridges linking the past and future
   old friends passing though with us still.
   Begin to the loneliness that cannot end
   since it perhaps is what makes us begin,
   begin to wonder at unknown faces
   at crying birds in the sudden rain
   at branches stark in the willing sunlight
   at seagulls foraging for bread
   at couples sharing a sunny secret

alone together while making good.
Though we live in a world that dreams of ending
that always seems about to give in
something that will not acknowledge conclusion
insists that we forever begin.

Brendan Kennelly, 'Begin'

acknowledgements

I n the preparation of this volume I have received much valuable help and advice from many generous friends and colleagues. My greatest debt is to Miss Poupak Moallem and Miss Sepedeh Hooshidari, who have been the chief co-ordinators of the whole project and without whose meticulous care and attention this anthology would not have been completed. I am also indebted to my students who have contributed in various ways to this anthology: Miss Kameh Bahrami, Miss Bita Farhoumand, Mr James Madaio, Miss Sukhmani Matharu, Miss Sukhna Matharu, Miss Elham Roohani, Mr Basir van de Fliert and Mr Nadim van de Fliert.

To the following I owe profound thanks for the valuable advice they have given me, the books with which they have provided me, and the comments they have made on the introduction and the compilation as a whole: Sir Marc Cochrane, Mr Shawn Doyle, Professor Brendan Kennelly, the Gaelic scholar Gearóid Ó Clérigh, Professor Susan Schreibman, Mr Colin Smythe, the poet Francis Warner and Dean and Professor Robert Welch.

I would also like to thank the staff of Oneworld Publications – Helen Coward, Rebecca Clare, Alex Ivey, Eoin Noble and Victoria Roddam – for all their hard work on this project.

A. P. Watt Limited on behalf of Michael B. Yeats for permission to publish

passages from *The Collected Works of W. B. Yeats*, vols I and II, edited by Richard
J. Finneran, David R. Clark and Rosalind E. Clark, *Essays and Introductions* by
W.B. Yeats, *Explorations* by W. B. Yeats compiled by Mrs W. B. Yeats, *Images and
Memories: A Pictorial Record of the Life and Work of W. B. Yeats*, edited by S. B.
Bushrui and J. M. Munro, *The Heart Grown Brutal: The Irish Revolution in
Literature, from Parnell to the Death of Yeats, 1891–1939* by Peter Costello, *Ideals
in Ireland* edited by Lady Gregory, *Literary Ideals in Ireland* by John Eglinton, W.
B. Yeats, A. E., and W. Larminie, *Prodigal Father: The Life of John Butler Yeats
(1839–1922)* by William M. Murphy, *The Senate Speeches of W. B. Yeats* edited
by Donald R. Pearce, *The Story of Anglo-Irish Poetry: 1800–1922* by Patrick
Power, *The Variorum Edition of the Poems of W. B. Yeats* edited by Peter Allt and
Russell K. Alspach, *Yeats's Verse Plays: The Revisions 1900–1910* by S. B. Bushrui.

Brendan Kennelly for permission to publish passages from *Begin* by Brendan
Kennelly and *The Penguin Book of Irish Verse* edited by Brendan Kennelly.

Colin Smythe Limited on behalf of the heirs of Diarmuid Russell for per-
mission to publish passages from *1000 Years of Irish Poetry* edited by
Kathleen Hoagland, *Collected Poems* by A. E. [George William Russell],
Ideals in Ireland edited by Lady Gregory, *Literary Ideals in Ireland* by John
Eglinton, W. B. Yeats, A. E., and W. Larminie, *The Descent of the Gods:
Comprising the Mystical Writings of G. W. Russell 'A. E.'* edited by Raghavan
Iyer and Nandini Iyer, *The Portable Irish Reader* edited by Diarmuid Russell,
Selections from the Irish Homestead, Vols 1 and 2.

Colin Smythe Limited on behalf of Veronica Jane O'Mara for permission
to publish passages from *The Collected Poems of Oliver St John Gogarty* by
Oliver St John Gogarty, *Perennial* by Oliver St John Gogarty, and *Wild
Apples* by Oliver St John Gogarty.

Colin Smythe Limited on behalf of Christina Bridgwater, Antonia Maria
Bridgwater, and Benedict Bridgwater for permission to publish passages from
The Autobiography of Maud Gonne: A Servant of the Queen edited by A. Norman
jeffares and Anna MacBride and *The Heart Grown Brutal: The Irish Revolution
in Literature, from Parnell to the Death of Yeats, 1891–1939* by Peter Costello.

David Higham Associates Limited for permission to publish passages
from *Irish Women Writers: An Uncharted Tradition* by Ann Owens Weekes.

The Department of Foreign Affairs for permission to publish passages from
Early Irish Lyrics: Eighth – Twelfth Century edited and translated by Gerard
Murphy, *The Ossianic Lore and Romantic Tales of Medieval Ireland* edited by
Gerard Murphy, *Saga and Myth in Ancient Ireland* by Gerard Murphy, *Early
Irish Poetry* edited by James Carney and *Irish Classical Poetry* by Eleanor Knott.

Desmond Egan for permission to publish passages from *Poems for Peace*.

Douglas Sealy for permission to publish passages from *1000 Years of Irish
Poetry* edited by Kathleen Hoagland, *A Literary History of Ireland: From
Earliest Times to the Present Day* by Douglas Hyde, and *Poems from the Irish*
by Douglas Hyde, edited by Monk Gibbon.

SOURCES

The following are the sources from which all the quotations in this anthology have been extracted.

A. E. [George William Russell]. *Collected Poems*. 1917. Reprint, St Clair Shores, MI: Scholarly Press, 1970.

—. *The Descent of the Gods: Comprising the Mystical Writings of G.W. Russell 'A. E.'*. Edited by Raghavan Iyer and Nandini Iyer. Collected Works of G. W. Russell – A. E., part 3. Gerrards Cross: Colin Smythe, 1988.

—. *Selections from the Contributions to 'The Irish Homestead'*. 2 Volumes. Edited by Henry Summerfield. Gerrards Cross: Colin Smythe, 1978.

Boucicault, Dion. *Plays by Dion Boucicault*. Edited by Peter Thomson. British and American Playwrights, 1750–1920. Cambridge: Cambridge University Press, 1984.

Bourniquel, Camille. *Ireland*. Translated by John Fisher. London: Vista Books,1960.

Bromage, Mary. 'Image of Nationhood'. *Éire–Ireland* 3, no. 3 (Autumn 1968). 11–26.

Burke, Edmund. *Selected Prose*. Edited by Sir Philip Magnus. London: Falcon Press, 1948.

—. *Selected Works*. Edited by W. J. Bate. New York: Random House, Modern Library, 1960.

Bushrui, S. B. *Yeats's Verse Plays: The Revisions 1900–1910*. Oxford: Clarendon Press, 1965.

Bushrui, S. B. and J. M. Munro, eds. *Images and Memories: A Pictorial Record of the Life and Work of W. B. Yeats.* Beirut: Dar el-Mashreq, 1970.

Byrne, Sandie, ed. *George Bernard Shaw's Plays.* 2nd edn New York: W. W. Norton and Co., 2002.

Cahill, Thomas. *How the Irish Saved Civilization.* New York: Bantam Doubleday Dell Publishing Group, Doubleday, Nan A. Talese, 1995.

Carney, James, ed. *Early Irish Poetry.* Dublin: Mercier Press for Radio Éireann, 1965.

—, trans. *Medieval Irish Lyrics.* Dublin: Dolmen Press, 1967.

Carty, Francis. *Irish Saints in Ten Countries.* Dublin: James Duffy & Co. Ltd., 1942.

Christensen, Lis and Lis Pihl, eds. *Ireland One: Risings and Troubles.* Copenhagen: Akademisk Forlag, 1981.

Colum, Padraic, ed. *The Poems of Samuel Ferguson.* Dublin: Allen Figgis, 1963.

—. *Three Plays.* Dublin: Allen Figgis, 1963.

Costello, Peter. *The Heart Grown Brutal: The Irish Revolution in Literature, from Parnell to the Death of Yeats, 1891–1939.* Dublin: Gill and Macmillan, 1977.

Curtin, Jeremiah. *Myths and Folktales of Ireland.* New York: Dover Publications, 1975.

Davis, Thomas. *Essays of Thomas Davis: Centenary Edition.* Edited by D. J. O'Donoghue. New York: Lemma Publishing, 1974.

de Jubainville, Henri d'Arbois. *Irish Mythological Cycle and Celtic Mythology.*Translated by Richard Irvine Best. Dublin: Hodges, Figgis, and Co., 1903.

Dillon, Myles, ed. *Early Irish Society.* Dublin: Colm O Lochlainn for the Cultural Relations Committee of Ireland, 1954.

—. *Irish Sagas.* Cork: Mercier Press, 1968.

Duckett, Eleanor Shipley. *The Gateway to the Middle Ages: Monasticism.* Ann Arbor: University of Michigan Press, Ann Arbor Paperbacks, 1961.

Duffy, Charles Gavan *et al. The Spirit of the Nation, 1845.* Poole, Dorset: Woodstock Books, 1998.

Dunsany, Lord. *The Donnellan Lectures, 1943.* London: William Heinemann, 1945.

Eakin, David B. and Michael Case, comps. *Selected Plays of George Moore and Edward Martyn,* Vol. 2 of Irish Drama Selections. Gerrards Cross: Colin Smythe, 1995.

Edgeworth, Maria. *Moral Tales.* London: Garland Publishing, Inc., 1974.

—. *The Parent's Assistant.* London: Garland Publishing, Inc., 1976.

Egan, Desmond. *Poems for Peace*. Dublin: The Goldsmith Press for Action From Ireland, 1986.

Eglinton, John, W. B. Yeats, A. E., and W. Larminie. *Literary Ideals in Ireland*. 1899. Reprint, New York: Lemma Publishing Corporation, 1973.

Facts About Ireland. Second Edition. Dublin: Department of External Affairs, 1969.

Fitzgibbon, Theodora. *A Taste of Ireland: Irish Traditional Food*. London: Pan Books, 1970.

Flanagan, Laurence, comp. *Irish Proverbs*. Dublin: Gill and Macmillan, 1995.

Foster, R.F. *Charles Stewart Parnell: The Man and his Family*. Hassocks, Sussex: The Harvester Press Limited; Atlantic Highlands, NJ: Humanities Press Inc., 1976.

Gogarty, Oliver St John. *The Collected Poems of Oliver St John Gogarty*. New York: Devin-Adair Company, 1954.

Gogarty, Oliver St John. *Distinguished Poets Series of Contemporary Poetry*. Edited by Mary Owings Miller. Vol. 1, Perennial. Baltimore, MD: Contemporary Poetry, 1944.

Gogarty, Oliver. *Wild Apples*. Dublin: Cuala Press, 1930.

Gregory, Lady. arr. and trans. *Cuchulain of Muirthemne: The Story of the Men of the Red Branch of Ulster*. The Coole Edition, Vol. 2. Gerrards Cross: Colin Smythe, 1970.

—. *Irish Folk-History Plays*, Second Series: The Tragic-Comedies.. New York: G.P. Putnam's Sons, 1912.

—. *The Collected Plays III: Wonder and the Supernatural*. The Coole Edition, Vol. 7 Gerrards Cross: Colin Smythe, 1971.

—. *The Kiltartan Books, comprising The Kiltartan Poetry, History, and Wonder Books*. The Coole Edition, Vol. 9. Gerrards Cross: Colin Smythe, 1971.

—. *A Book of Saints and Wonders*. The Coole Edition, Vol. 12. Gerrards Cross, Bucks.: Colin Smythe, 1971.

—. *Our Irish Theatre: A Chapter of Autobiography*. New York: G. P. Putnam's Sons, 1914.

—. *Poets and Dreamers: Studies and Translations from the Irish*. The Coole Edition, Vol. 11. Gerrards Cross: Colin Smythe, 1974.

—. *Visions and Beliefs in the West of Ireland*. The Coole Edition. New York: Oxford University Press, 1970.

—, ed. *Ideals in Ireland*. 1901. Reprint, NY: Lemma Publishing Corp., 1973.

—, trans. and arr. *Gods and Fighting Men*. The Coole Edition. New York: Oxford University Press, 1970.

Hare, Augustus J. C., ed. *The Life and Letters of Maria Edgeworth*. Volume II. 1894. Reprint, Freeport, New York: Books for Libraries Press, 1971.

Healy, James N. *Percy French and His Songs*. Cork: Mercier Press in association with Herbert Jenkins, 1966.

Heaney, Seamus. *Electric Light*. New York: Farrar, Straus and Giroux, 2001.

Henry, Françoise. *Irish High Crosses*. Dublin: Cultural Relations Committee, 1964.

Hewitt, John, ed. *The Poems of William Allingham*. An Chomhairle Ealaíon Series of Irish Authors. Dublin: Dolmen Press, 1967.

Hoagland, Kathleen, ed. *1000 Years of Irish Poetry*. Old Saybrook, CT: Konecky and Konecky by special arrangement with Devin-Adair Company, 1975.

Hurst, Michael. *Parnell and Irish Nationalism*. London: Routledge & Kegan Paul, 1968.

Hyde, Douglas. *A Literary History of Ireland: From Earliest Times to the Present Day*. The Library of Literary History. London: T. Fisher Unwin, 1899.

—. *Poems from the Irish*. Edited by Monk Gibbon. An Chomhairle Ealaíon Series of Irish Authors, Number 4. Dublin: Allen Figgis, 1963.

Irish Digest, The. Vol. 89, no. 2. (May 1967).

Irish Sayings. Bath: Paragon, Tara, 1999.

Jeffares, A. Norman and Anna MacBride White, eds. *The Autobiography of Maud Gonne: A Servant of the Queen*. Chicago: The University of Chicago Press, 1994.

Joyce, P. W., trans. *Old Celtic Romances*. The Sackville Library Edition. Dublin: Gill and Macmillan Ltd, 1978.

Keefe, Joan, trans. *Irish Poems: from Cromwell to the Famine*. Lewisburg, PA: Bucknell University Press, 1977.

Kennelly, Brendan. *Begin*. Newcastle upon Tyne: Bloodaxe Books, 1999.

—, ed. *The Penguin Book of Irish Verse*. Harmondsworth: Penguin Books, 1970.

Kinsella, Thomas, trans. *The Tain*. Dublin: Dolmen Press, 1969; Reprint, Philadelphia: University of Pennsylvania Press, 1985.

—, ed. and trans., *The New Oxford Book of Irish Verse*. Oxford: Oxford University Press, 1986.

Knott, Eleanor. *Irish Classical Poetry: Commonly Called Bardic Poetry*. 2nd edn. Irish Life and Culture, Vol. 6. Dublin: Colm O Lochlainn for the Cultural Relations Committee of Ireland, 1960.

Littlefield, Hazel. *Lord Dunsany: King of Dreams, a Personal Portrait*. New York: Exposition Press, 1959.

Longford, Earl of and Thomas P. O'Neill. *Eamon de Valera*. Dublin: Gill and Macmillan in association with Hutchinson of London, 1970.

Luce, A. A. and T. E. Jessop. *The Works of George Berkeley: Bishop of Cloyne*. Volumes 1–9. London: Thomas Nelson and Sons, 1948–57.

Lucy, Seán, ed. *Love Poems of the Irish*. Cork: Mercier Press, 1967.

Lyons, David. *Land of the Poets: Ireland*. London: Greenwich Editions, 2002.

MacAonghusa, Proinsias, comp. *Quotations from P. H. Pearse*. Dublin: Mercier Press, 1979.

McCann, Sean, comp. *The Wit of the Irish*. London: Leslie Frewin Publishers, 1968.

Macardle, Dorothy. *The Irish Republic*. London: Corgi Books, a division of Transworld Publishers, 1968.

Mac Con Iomaire, Liam. *Ireland of the Proverb*. Dublin: Town House and Country House, 1988.

MacDonagh, Donagh and Lennox Robinson, comps. *The Oxford Book of Irish Verse: XVIIth Century–XXth Century*. Oxford: Clarendon Press, 1959.

MacHale, Des, comp. *Irish Wit*. Cork: Mercier Press, 2002.

McMahon, Sean, ed. *Irish Quotations*. Dublin: O'Brien Press, 1987.

—, comp. *A Little Book of Irish Quotations*. Belfast: Appletree Press, 1994.

MacManus, M. J., ed. *Thomas Davis and Young Ireland*. Dublin: Stationery Office, 1945.

MacManus, Seumas. *The Story of the Irish Race: A Popular History of Ireland*. 2nd edn. New York: Irish Publishing, 1922.

Madden, Daniel Owen, ed. *Speeches of the Right Hon. Henry Grattan*. 2nd edn. Dublin: James Duffy, 1853.

Mangan, James Clarence. *Autobiography*. Edited by James Kilroy. Dublin: Dolmen Press, 1968.

Meyer, Kuno, trans. *Selections from Ancient Irish Poetry*. London: Constable and Co., 1911.

Molyneux, William. *The Case of Ireland*. 1698. Reprint, with introduction by J. G. Simms and afterword by Denis Donoghue. Irish Writings from the Age of Swift, Vol. 5. Dublin: Cadenus Press, 1977.

Moore, George. *Celibate Lives*. The Landmark Library, no. 2. London: Chatto & Windus, 1968.

—. *Esther Waters*. London: Oxford University Press, 1964.

—. *'Hail and Farewell!': Salve*. London: William Heinemann, 1937.

Moore, Thomas. *Poems*. Edinburgh: William P. Nimmo, n.d.

—. *The Poetical Works of Thomas Moore*. Boston: Phillips, Sampson, and Company, 1859.

Morgan, Lady. *Woman and her Master*. 1840. Reprint, Hyperion reprint series: Pioneers of the Woman's Movement. Westport, CT: Hyperion Press, Inc., 1976.

Murphy, Gerard. *Saga and Myth in Ancient Ireland*. Irish Life and Culture, Vol. 10. Dublin: Colm O Lochlainn for the Cultural Relations Committee of Ireland, 1961.

—, ed. and trans. *Early Irish Lyrics: Eighth–Twelfth Century*. Oxford: Oxford University Press, Clarendon Press, 1956.

—, ed. *The Ossianic Lore and Romantic Tales of Medieval Ireland*. Irish Life and Culture, Vol. 11. Dublin: Colm O Lochlainn for the Cultural Relations Committee of Ireland, 1961.

Murphy, Maureen O'Rourke and James MacKillop. *Irish Literature: A Reader*. Irish Studies. Syracuse, NY: Syracuse University Press, 1987.

Murphy, William M. *Prodigal Father: The Life of John Butler Yeats (1839–1922)*. Ithaca, NY: Cornell University Press, 1978.

Ní Dhomhnaill, Nuala. *Pharoah's Daughter*. Winston-Salem, NC: Wake Forest University Press, 1993.

O'Brien, Flann. *The Poor Mouth: A Bad Story about the Hard Life*. New York: Seaver Books, The Viking Press, Inc., 1981.

—. *The Third Policeman*. Normal: Dalkey Archive Press, 1999.

O'Brien, Siobhan, ed. *Irish Songs*. New Lanark, Scotland: Lagan Books, Geddes and Grosset, 2002.

Ó Clérigh, Gearóid. 'Patience'. *The Recorder*, published by The American Irish Historical Society. (1978).

—. *Ál Fiaich*. Dublin: An Clóchomhar, 1975.

—. *Creach Coigríche agus Cnuas Cois Trá*. Dublin: Coiscéim., 2003.

O'Connell, Maurice R. 'Daniel O'Connell and Irish Americans'. *Éire-Ireland* 16, no. 2 (Summer 1981): 7–15.

O'Connor, Frank [Michael O'Donovan]. *The Fountain of Magic*. London: Macmillan and Co., 1939; Ann Arbor, MI: University Microfilms, a Xerox Company, 1970.

O'Faolain, Sean. *The Irish: A Character Study*. New York: Devin-Adair Company, 1949.

O'Flanagan, Theophilus. *Transactions of the Gaelic Society*. Dublin: Gaelic Society, 1851.

O'Grady, Standish James. *Early Bardic Literature, Ireland. 1879*. Reprint, New York: Lemma Publishing Corp., 1970.

O'Shea, Katharine (Mrs. Charles Stewart Parnell). *Charles Stewart Parnell: His Love Story and Political Life*. Vol 2. Second Impression. London: Cassell and Company, 1914.

O'Sullivan, Sean. *Legends from Ireland*. London: B. T. Batsford, 1977.

Ó Tuama, Seán, ed. *An Duanaire: 1600–1900: Poems of the Dispossessed*. Translated by Thomas Kinsella. Dolmen Press in association with Mountrath, Portlaoise, Ireland: Bord na Gaeilge, 1981

Pearse, Padraic. *The Murder Machine, and other essays.* Dublin: Mercier Press, 1976.

Power, Patrick. *The Story of Anglo-Irish Poetry: 1800–1922.* Cork: Mercier Press, 1967.

Rafroidi, Patrick. *Irish Literature in English: The Romantic Period (1789–1850)*, Vol. 1. Gerrards Cross: Colin Smythe, 1980.

Rolleston, T. W. *Myths and Legends of the Celtic Race.* Second and Revised Edition. London: George G. Harp & Co., 1911.

Russell, Diarmuid, ed. *The Portable Irish Reader.* New York: Viking Press, 1946.

Schreibman, Susan. *Collected Poems of Thomas MacGreevy: An Annotated Edition.* Dublin: Anna Livia Press, Washington, DC: The Catholic University of America Press, 1991.

Seoighe, Mainchín, ed. *The Irish Quotation Book: A Literary Companion.* London: Robert Hale, 1992.

Shannon, Ashley, comp. *Irish Blessings: A Photographic Celebration.* Philadelphia: Running Press, Courage Books, 1999.

Shaw, Bernard. *Nine Plays.* New York: Dodd, Mead & Co., 1931.

Sheridan, Richard Brinsley. *The Dramatic Works of Richard Brinsley Sheridan.* Edited by Cecil Price. Vol. 2. Oxford: Clarendon Press, 1973.

—. *The Plays & Poems of Richard Brinsley Sheridan.* Edited by R. Crompton Rhodes. New York: Russell & Russell, 1962.

Sigerson, George. *Bards of the Gael and Gall.* 1925. Reprint, New York: Lemma Publishing Corp., 1974.

Stephens, James. *Collected Poems of James Stephens.* New York: Macmillan Company, 1926.

—. *The Crock of Gold.* New York: Macmillan Company, 1913.

Sullivan, T. D., A. M. Sullivan and D. B. Sullivan, eds. *Speeches from the Dock.* Dublin: Gill and Macmillan, 1968.

Swift, Jonathan. *A Proposal for Correcting the English Tongue: Polite Conversations, etc.* Edited by Herbert Davis with Louis Landa. Oxford: Basil Blackwell, 1964.

Synge, John M. *Collected Works.* 4 volumes. Edited by Robin Skelton. London: Oxford University Press, 1962–8.

Taylor, Geoffrey, comp. *Irish Poets of the Nineteenth Century.* London: Routledge & Kegan Paul, 1951. Reprint, Westport, CT: Greenwood Press, 1971.

Townshend, George. *The Genius of Ireland and other essays.* Dublin: Talbot Press, 1930.

Tynan, Katherine. *The Poems of Katherine Tynan.* Edited by Monk Gibbon. An Chomhairle Ealaíon Series of Irish Authors, Number 6. Dublin: Allen Figgis, 1963.

Warner, Charles Dudley, ed. *Library of the World's Best Literature: Ancient and Modern*. 46 vols. New York: J. A. Hill & Company, 1902.

Weekes, Ann Owens. *Irish Women Writers: An Uncharted Tradition*. Lexington, KY: University Press of Kentucky, 1990.

Wilde, Jane Francesca (Elgee) Lady. *Ancient Legends, Mystic Charms and Superstitions of Ireland: With Sketches of the Irish Past*. 1925. Reprint, New York: Lemma Publishing Corp., 1973.

Wilde, Oscar. *Complete Poetry*. Edited by Isobel Murray. Oxford: Oxford University Press, 1997.

—. *I Can Resist Everything Except Temptation and Other Quotations from Oscar Wilde*. Compiled by Karl Beckson. New York: Columbia University Press, 1996.

—. *The Complete Works of Oscar Wilde*. Edited by F. B. Foreman. London: Collins, 1966.

—. *The Poems and Fairy Tales of Oscar Wilde*. The Modern Library of the World's Best Books. New York: Random House, n.d.

—. *The Soul of Man under Socialism and other Essays*. New York: Harper Colophon Books, Harper & Row, 1970.

Woodham-Smith, Cecil. *The Great Hunger: Ireland, 1845–1849*. New York: Signet Books, New American Library, 1962.

Yeats, W. B. *Explorations*. Compiled by Mrs W. B. Yeats. New York: Collier Books, 1973.

—. *The Senate Speeches of W. B. Yeats*. Edited by Donald R. Pearce. London: Faber and Faber, 1961.

—. *The Variorum Edition of the Poems of W. B. Yeats*. Edited by Peter Allt and Russell K. Alspach. New York: Macmillan, 1957.

—. *Essays and Introductions*. New York: The MacMillan Company, 1961.

—. *The Collected Works of W. B. Yeats*. Edited by Richard J. Finneran and George Mills Harper. Vol. 1, The Poems: Revised. Edited by Richard J. Finneran. New York: Macmillan Publishing Company, 1989.

—. *The Collected Works of W. B. Yeats*. Edited by Richard J. Finneran and George Mills Harper. Vol. 2, The Plays. Edited by David R. Clark and Rosalind E. Clark. New York: Scribner, 2001.

index